THE ROMANS

Written and illustrated by
Emma Karolyi

First published
November 2002 in Great Britain
by

Educational Printing Services Limited
Albion Mill, Water Street, Great Harwood, Blackburn BB6 7QR
Telephone: (01254) 882080   Fax: (01254) 882010
e-mail: enquiries@eprint.co.uk   web site: www.eprint.co.uk

ISBN 1 900818 08 6

© Emma Karolyi 2002

This Master may only be reproduced by the original purchaser for use with his/her class(es).
The publisher prohibits the loaning or onselling of this Master for the purposes of reproduction.

INTRODUCTION

The Roman Empire was one of the most important empires in history, lasting over a thousand years, from its founding in 753 B.C. to its fall in A.D. 476. Under the reigns of the emperors, Rome's influence spread and the empire expanded through the conquering force of the powerful Roman army. Rights and privileges of citizenship, government, security and a sophisticated justice system also attracted countries to ally themselves with Rome. It was an empire that united a large number of countries under one rule - something that has not been repeated in history on such a large scale. Despite the fall of the empire, Roman civilisation has had an enormous impact and influence on subsequent cultures.

The Romans is a set of worksheets aimed at the upper primary age range and written to support the curriculum schemes. The worksheets offer geographical and historical research skill opportunities in particular, as well as providing a broad overview of the everyday life of Romans, of their technological innovations and the impact of the Roman period on the present day.

A wide range of activities covers topics from the foundation of Rome and aspects of Roman life, such as the army, houses, education, fashion, food and drink, to the legacy of Rome. Britain at the time of the Romans and the interaction of Celtic and Roman life are comprehensively covered through varied and adaptable research-based tasks. A number of primary sources are included in the activities, to allow children to have first-hand accounts of the time and to encourage them to interpret and draw conclusions about events and people, their beliefs and their values.

Particular emphasis is given to geographical studies: the scope of Roman settlement in the Italian peninsula and in Britain, and the spread of the empire throughout the Roman period, comparing the achievements of key emperors through inventive and stimulating map work, encouraging comparison with present geographical features, developing pupils' understanding of, among other things, the Romans' contribution to modern town planning and road building in Britain.

The comprehensive teachers' notes present detailed background information for the teacher and suggestions on how to use each activity. Curriculum links are given for each activity - the relevant pages are marked beside the key elements in the grids, for both the National Curriculum of England and the 5 - 14 guidelines for Scotland, to enable easy cross-referencing and planning.

ACKNOWLEDGEMENTS

I would particularly like to thank the following people who played an important role in supporting me with this book: John Foster, my father, who lent me so much reference material from his study, Chris Houghton, my nephew, who helped me to test out and refine the technology activities and who invented his version of the shooting ballista, which features in this book, Ken and Heather Goodare, my parents-in-law, who proof-read the whole text, and above all to Julian, my husband, who supported and encouraged me all the way and who spent hours scanning the illustrations.

THIS BOOK IS DEDICATED TO JULIAN AND THOMAS.

CONTENTS

Who were the Romans?	1
How to make a History Detective Wheel	2
Roman Primary Sources	3
Archaeological Dig	5
Roman Timeline	7
Where is Italy?	9
The City of Rome	12
The Story of Romulus and Remus	13
Where would you have built a city like Rome?	16
The Roman Emperors	18
Celtic Britain - A Mini Study	19
Roman Army	33
Julius Caesar	45
Emperor Claudius	48
Boudicca	50
Hadrian's Wall	53
Roman Britain Timeline	57
Maps to show growth of Roman Invasion	58
Roman Roads	60
Roman Towns in Britain	65
Roman Architecture	72
Roman Houses	75
Roman Villas	78
Roman Gardens	83
Roman Citizens	84
Children and Education	87
Roman Numerals	88
Latin Language	89
Money and Trade	90
Roman Clothing	91
Roman Fashion	93
Food and Drink	94
Entertainment	96
Roman Baths	100
Roman Religion	103
Death and Burial	111
The Collapse of the Roman Empire	113
What has changed and what has stayed the same?	115
The Legacy of Ancient Rome	116
Teachers' Notes	117
Historical References	152
Geographical References	154
Design Technology	156

WHO WERE THE ROMANS?

The Romans lived over 2000 years ago. Unfortunately this was before there were any cameras or videos, so how do we know so much about the Romans and the way that they lived?

A person who finds out about the past is called a HISTORIAN. Professor Oliver Strigil looks in many places and at objects to help him to find out what life was like over 2000 years ago, in Roman times.

Some of these places and objects are:

1. _____ 2. _____

3. _____ 4. _____

5. _____ 6. _____

These things are called **SOURCES**. Piecing together what life was like in the past is why historians enjoy their work. It is like doing a difficult jigsaw, fitting together the pieces, or being a detective, trying to work out what happened and looking for clues. Sometimes historians can be sure about something, but at other times what happened in history remains a mystery. The only thing then is to guess.

Primary sources of evidence
- evidence that comes from Roman times. E.g. A Roman mosaic or a coin. Historians have to ask many questions and interpret what they find.

Secondary sources of evidence
- evidence that does not come from the time but is **about** the time of the Romans. E.g. A book or a video about the Romans.

Using your six ideas above, make a History Detective Wheel (see next page), showing the different ways that we could find out about life in Roman times, two thousand years ago.

HOW TO MAKE A HISTORY DETECTIVE WHEEL

1. Carefully cut out the two circles A and B.

2. Cut out the window on circle A.

3. Draw in your sources of evidence into the triangular sections of circle B.

4. Attach the two circles together with a split pin.

5. You may like to write the names of your sources around the edge, on wheel B.

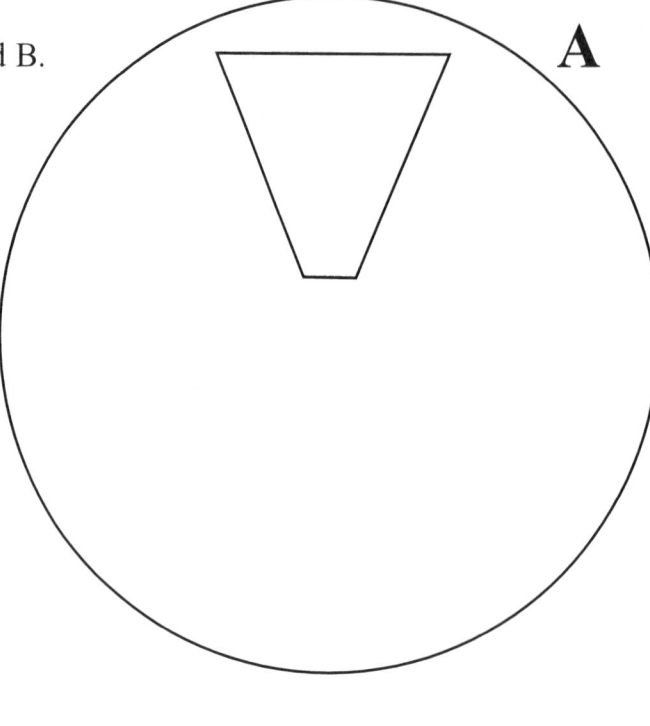

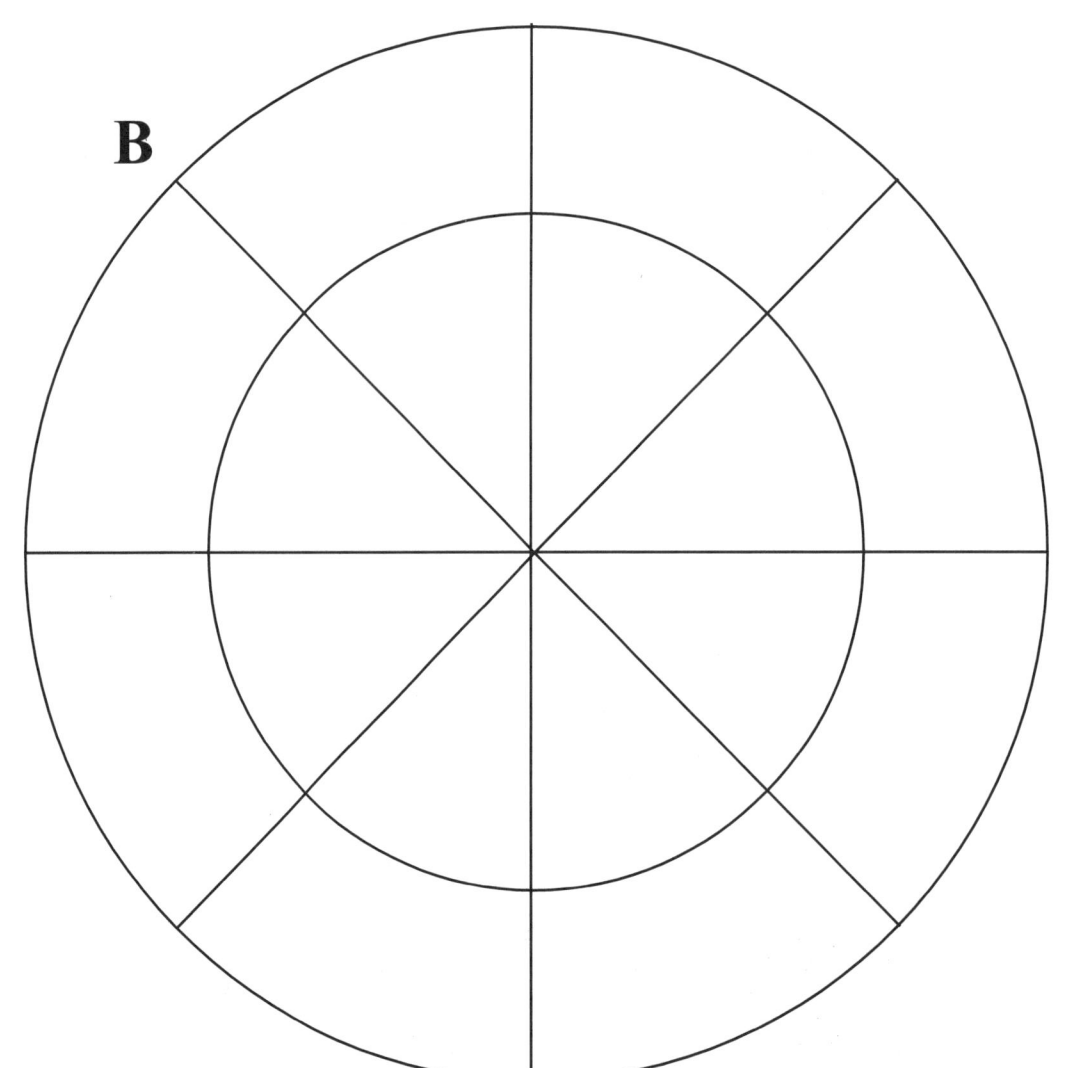

ROMAN PRIMARY SOURCES I
Many of the following are still intact today

Draw and label as many Roman pictures as you can under the five categories.

1. BUILDINGS - such as villas and temples, tell us about the style of architecture. Ruins of roads and aqueducts also tell us more about the Romans.

2. SCULPTURES, MOSAICS, and WALL PAINTINGS - these tell us about the way the Romans decorated their public buildings and homes.

3. OBJECTS (tools, toys, coins, utensils etc.) - these are well preserved and give us information about what everyday items the Romans used.

ROMAN PRIMARY SOURCES II

4. WRITING (history, politics, poems, plays, military records and letters) - little has survived but what is left tells us about the lives and characters of the people of Rome.

5. STONE INSCRIPTIONS (laws, military records, financial transactions, graves)

Write down some reasons why you think historians have to be careful in drawing conclusions about Roman life, when using primary sources like these above:

ARCHAEOLOGICAL DIG I

1. *Find out what ARCHAEOLOGY is and what an ARCHAEOLOGIST does. Write it here:*

Archaeologists use a number of different tools to do their job. What they use depends on the object that they are excavating and where it is.

2. *Label the tool, using the words below.*

A. _____

B. _____

C. _____

D. _____

E. _____

F. _____

SPADE • TROWEL • TOOTHBRUSH • PICK

WHEELBARROW • MEASURING TAPE

3. *Try to match the job to the correct tool.*

This tool is used to remove layers of earth gently: _____

This tool is used to scoop the earth into D: _____

This tool is used to remove dirt from delicate objects: _____

This tool is used to loosen the earth: _____

This tool is used to cart the soil away: _____

This tool is used to measure the site and objects: _____

ARCHAEOLOGICAL DIG II

Archaeology is one way of learning about people from the past.

4. *You are going to be an archaeologist on an archeological dig. Dig down and unscramble the words to reveal what Roman remains you have found buried. Be careful to use the correct tools!*

        KLEENOTS   **BREALM**

        PREMUFE TELBOT   **NIEW GUJ**

        DOLG TRABECLE   **STIEL**

5. *Sketch the objects that you have revealed above.*

BE A DETECTIVE:

6. Look at the Roman remains that you have uncovered.
Write down what they reveal about the person who was buried here.

ROMAN TIMELINE I

Write the following important Roman dates onto Roman Timeline Sheet II. Be careful to write them in the correct place! The first one has been done for you.

753 BC   -   ROME IS FOUNDED

510 BC   -   ROMAN REPUBLIC BEGINS

59-49 BC -   JULIUS CAESAR CONQUERS GAUL

55 BC   -   JULIUS CAESAR INVADES BRITAIN

44 BC   -   JULIUS CAESAR IS ASSASSINATED

27 BC   -   EMPERORS RULE ROME

AD 61   -   BOUDICCA IS DEFEATED

AD 122   -   HADRIAN BECOMES EMPEROR

AD 410   -   ROMANS WITHDRAW FROM BRITAIN

ROMAN TIMELINE II

Below is a timeline showing Roman times. Use the dates from 'Roman Timeline I' to complete the timeline.

B.C.

800

753 B.C. Rome is founded

600

400

200

Birth of Christ

200

A.D.

400

600

1. What does A.D. stand for?

2. What does this mean?

3. What does B.C. stand for?

4. What does this mean?

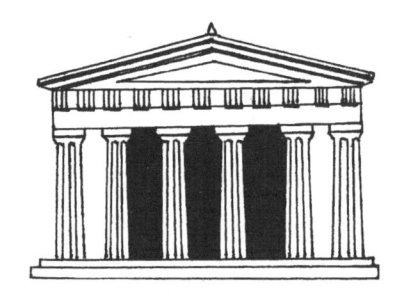

WHERE IS ITALY?

Using an atlas, find a map of Italy and complete the questions below:

1. Look for Rome in your atlas and label it in its correct place on the map below.

2. Using coloured pencils, colour the sea blue and the land green.

3. Mark the seven hills which surround Rome in brown. Write down the names of some of them in the space below:

4. On the map, write down the seas which surround Italy.

5. Ancient Rome was called ROMA. The people were called Romans. What language did they speak?

6. Find out how the Ancient Romans travelled around their empire.

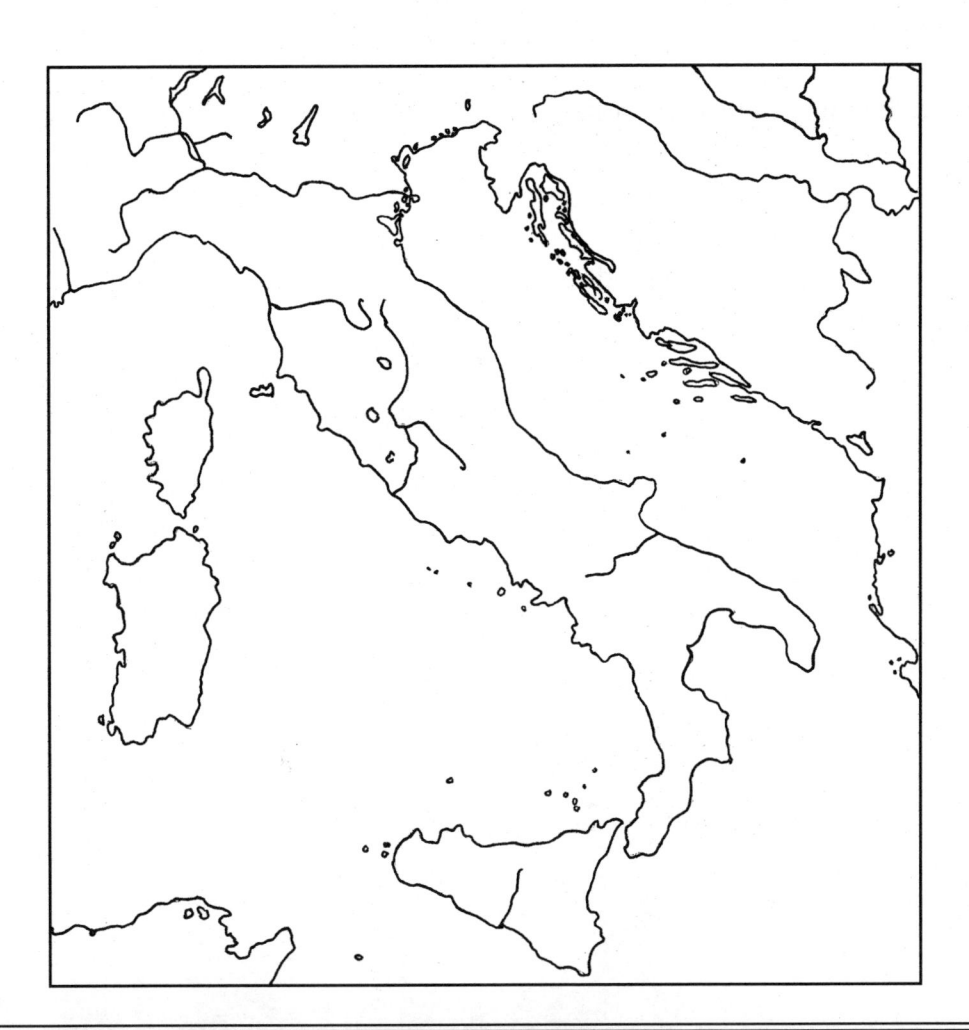

WHERE IN THE WORLD IS MODERN ITALY?

In groups, brainstorm what you know about Modern Italy.

LET'S RESEARCH MODERN ITALY
Use reference books to help you answer these questions about Italy:

1. In which continent is Italy?

2. What is the capital city of Italy?

3. Colour the Italian flag:

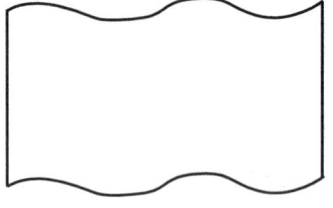

4. Name three famous towns or cities in Italy:

5. What is the currency used in modern Italy?

6. How many people live in Italy today?

7. What are the main industries in Italy?

8. What language is spoken in modern Italy?

9. Think of three reasons why people visit modern Italy.

10. Which food and drinks come from Italy? Draw and label them below:

WHERE IN THE WORLD IS ANCIENT ITALY?

In groups, brainstorm what you know about Ancient Italy.

LET'S RESEARCH ANCIENT ITALY
Use reference books to find out about Ancient Italy to help you answer these questions:

1. In which continent was Ancient Italy?

2. What was the capital city of Ancient Italy?

3. Find out and draw any city symbols which the Ancient Romans had:

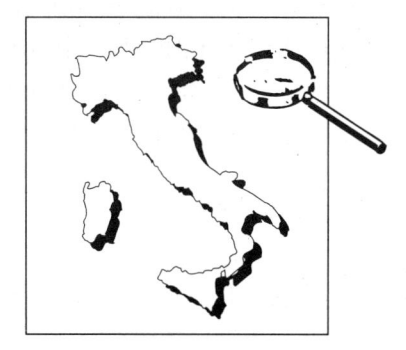

4. Name three famous towns or cities in Ancient Italy:

5. What kind of money did the Ancient Romans use?

6. Find out what the population of Ancient Rome was.

7. What did the Ancient Romans invent?

8. What language was spoken in Ancient Italy? Find out some words in this language:

9. Try to find out what the Romans called the following:
   Mediterranean Sea, Britain, Spain, France.

10. Find out what food the Ancient Romans ate. Did they differ from modern Italian foods? Draw and label them below:

THE CITY OF ROME

THE FOUNDING

From about 2000 BC, many migrants from Central Europe (including a group called the Latins) settled in the northwest of Italy. They settled in a cluster of villages built on seven hills, which surrounded a plain. There was plenty of fertile agricultural land and it was near to a river. Eventually the villages merged together and spread onto this plain. Traditionally the date of the city of Rome's founding was 753 B.C. The plain became known as Latium, and the river, the River Tiber.

THE LEGEND

Little is known about the origin of Rome. One legend, written by a Roman called Virgil, tells the story of a man named Aeneas who escaped from Troy at the end of the Trojan war and who sailed to Italy. Livy, another Roman author, wrote 'The Early History of Rome'. He wrote about how Aeneas landed in Italy, befriended King Latinus and married his daughter Lavinia. Later, Aeneas' son Ascanius founded a city called Alba Longa and became the first of many kings to rule there for the next 400 years. When the last king was overthrown, his twin grandsons Romulus and Remus were left to die beside the River Tiber by a wicked uncle. A she-wolf found them and suckled them. When they grew up they discovered who they were and what had happened and they killed their wicked uncle. After a fight between the two brothers, Romulus became the first king of Rome and the city was named after him.

1. *Name two Roman authors who wrote about the origins of Rome.*

2. *Why did people choose to settle in the Northwest of Italy?*

3. *Statues of Romulus and Remus and the she-wolf can be found all over Rome and other Italian cities today. Sketch this statue.*

THE STORY OF ROMULUS AND REMUS

Read the full story of Romulus and Remus.

A king named Numitor once ruled Rome. His younger brother Amulius however overpowered him and took the throne for himself. Amulius killed his nephews but not his beautiful niece Rhea Silvia. She was a priestess of the goddess Vesta. As a priestess of Vesta she had sworn a promise never to marry or have children. This meant that she was not a threat to her wicked uncle, Amulius. However, one day the god Mars fell in love with Rhea Silvia. Sometime later, Rhea Silvia bore twin sons called Romulus and Remus.

Rhea Silvia had broken her promise to the goddess Vesta and her uncle became angry. She was thrown into prison and servants were ordered to take the babies and drown them in the River Tiber so they would not be a threat to his rule.

The servants did as they were told but instead left the babies on the riverside, believing they would perish. A mother wolf found them and fed them with her milk. The wolf looked after them until a shepherd called Faustulus and his wife Larentia discovered them and brought them up as their own children.

Faustulus had long suspected that they were of royal blood and when the boys grew up, he told them the story. This was confirmed by Numitor. Realising the truth, Romulus and Remus killed their wicked uncle Amulius and placed their grandfather Numitor back on the throne.

Some time later, Romulus and Remus built a city on the spot where they had been found. However, the brothers could not decide what to name this new city. Both Romulus and Remus thought it should be named after themselves. They argued bitterly and had a fight. Romulus killed his brother Remus and therefore called the new city Rome after himself.

You may like to act this story of Romulus and Remus in groups

CHARACTERS

Narrator	Mars, God of War
Numitor, King of Rome	Romulus
Amulius, the evil brother	Remus
2 Nephews	Mother Wolf
2 servants	Faustulus
Rhea Vesta	Larentia

Make a series of drawings with captions, like a filmstrip, to explain the story of Romulus and Remus.

THE STORY OF ROMULUS AND REMUS

THE STORY OF ROMULUS AND REMUS

WHERE WOULD YOU HAVE BUILT A CITY LIKE ROME?

Imagine that you are Romulus and you want to choose a place to build a city. What natural features can you think of that should be near by?

Write down the advantages and disadvantages of living near to the following natural features:

Natural Features	Advantages	Disadvantages
Forest		
Water River Spring		
Poor Soil		
Hills		
Marsh land		
Good Soil		

WHERE WOULD YOU HAVE BUILT A CITY LIKE ROME?

Thinking about the advantages and disadvantages of natural features when building a city, design a plan of a place where you could safely build a city. The river and two hills have already been drawn for you. You will need to add marshland, areas with good and poor soil, forests and more hills (if you wish). Mark the city in red.

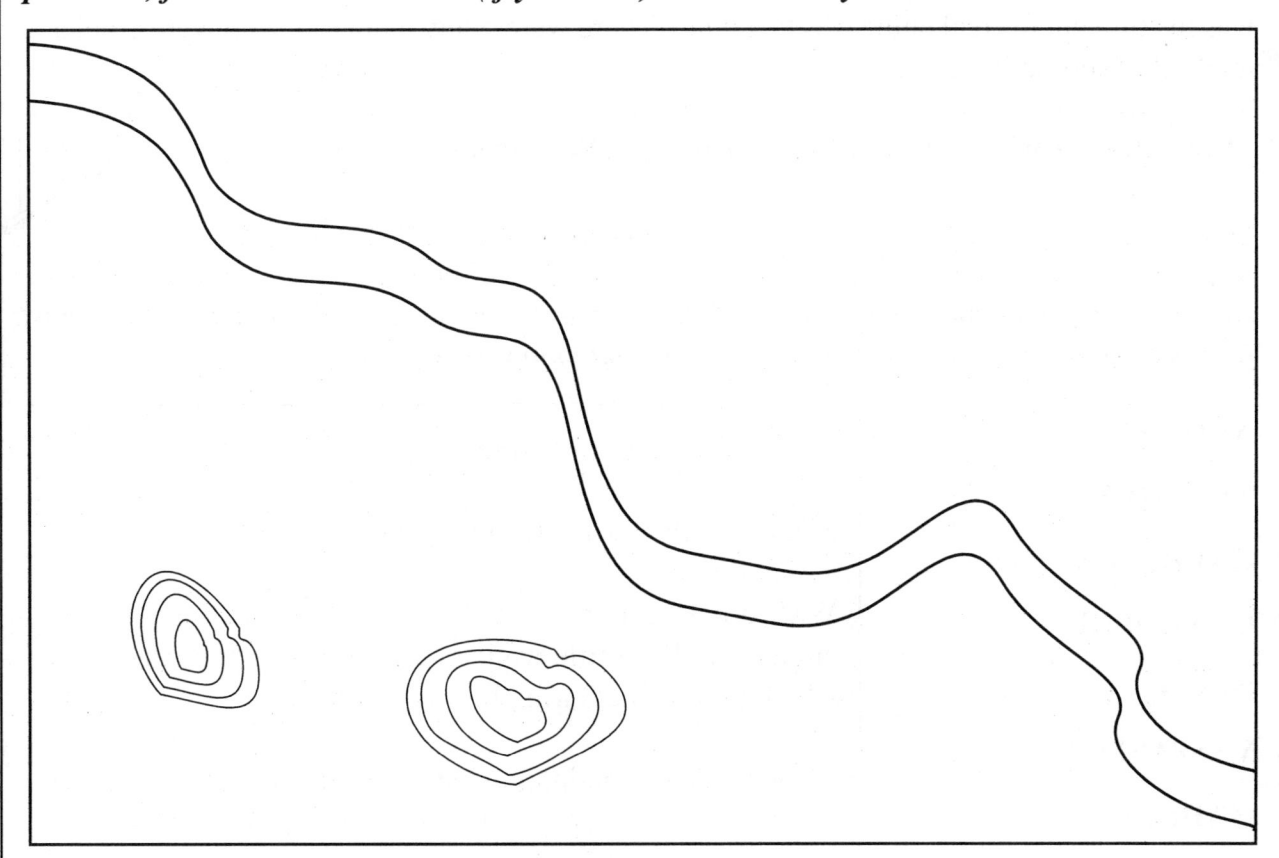

Fill in the key with your own symbols and colours.

KEY	
Forest	
Marsh	
River	~~~
Good Soil	
Poor Soil	
Hills	◎

Look closely at your map plan. An official city planner is coming to inspect it. How would you justify where you are going to build your city and convince him / her that it is in the right place? Make notes below to help you think what you would say.

THE ROMAN EMPERORS

There were about eighty-five emperors who ruled Rome. They used the title 'Caesar', after Julius Caesar.

Julius Caesar's adopted son became the first Emperor. He was called Augustus Caesar. This was his title but his real name was Octavian. There were many emperors who were cruel and mad, like Nero and Caligula.

FIND OUT - what the Latin word IMPERATOR means:

In pairs or small groups, find out as much as you can about one or more of the following emperors listed below: when they ruled, what they achieved and what they are most famous for. Read the box below to give you some more ideas.

AUGUSTUS

TIBERIUS

CALIGULA

CLAUDIUS

NERO

VESPASIAN

HADRIAN

TRAJAN

SEPTIMIUS SEVERUS

DIOCLETIAN

CONSTANTINE

JULIAN

More ideas for research:

Make a birth certificate and draw his family tree.

Write a newspaper report about something that this emperor did (a battle won, a building built, a disaster which took place during his reign etc.)

A short letter explaining what life is like under his rule. You could be a soldier in the army, a citizen, a Roman lady or an educated slave.

A map of the empire during his reign.

A document of his achievements.

An obituary of the emperor. (Ask your teacher if you don't know what this is).

Illustrations, pictures etc.

Did you know?

In *very* recent history, the title 'Caesar' has been used for rulers of different countries. Germany used the word KAISER, Iran used the word SHAH and Russia used the word TSAR.

FIND OUT - what official colour did the Emperor wear?
- what would an emperor do with laurels and why?

Celtic Britain

Life in Britain before the Roman Invasion.

A Mini Study

Celtic Britain 1 - A Mini Study

Who were the Celts?

The Celts lived in Britain before the Romans invaded. Many of them arrived from the eastern side of Europe in about 7000 B.C. and built settlements here. They were skilled workers and farmers and were divided into tribes. Each tribe had its own ruler or chief and they were loyal to him or her. The warriors, chiefs and servants lived in a hill fort, which was protected by high wooden walls.

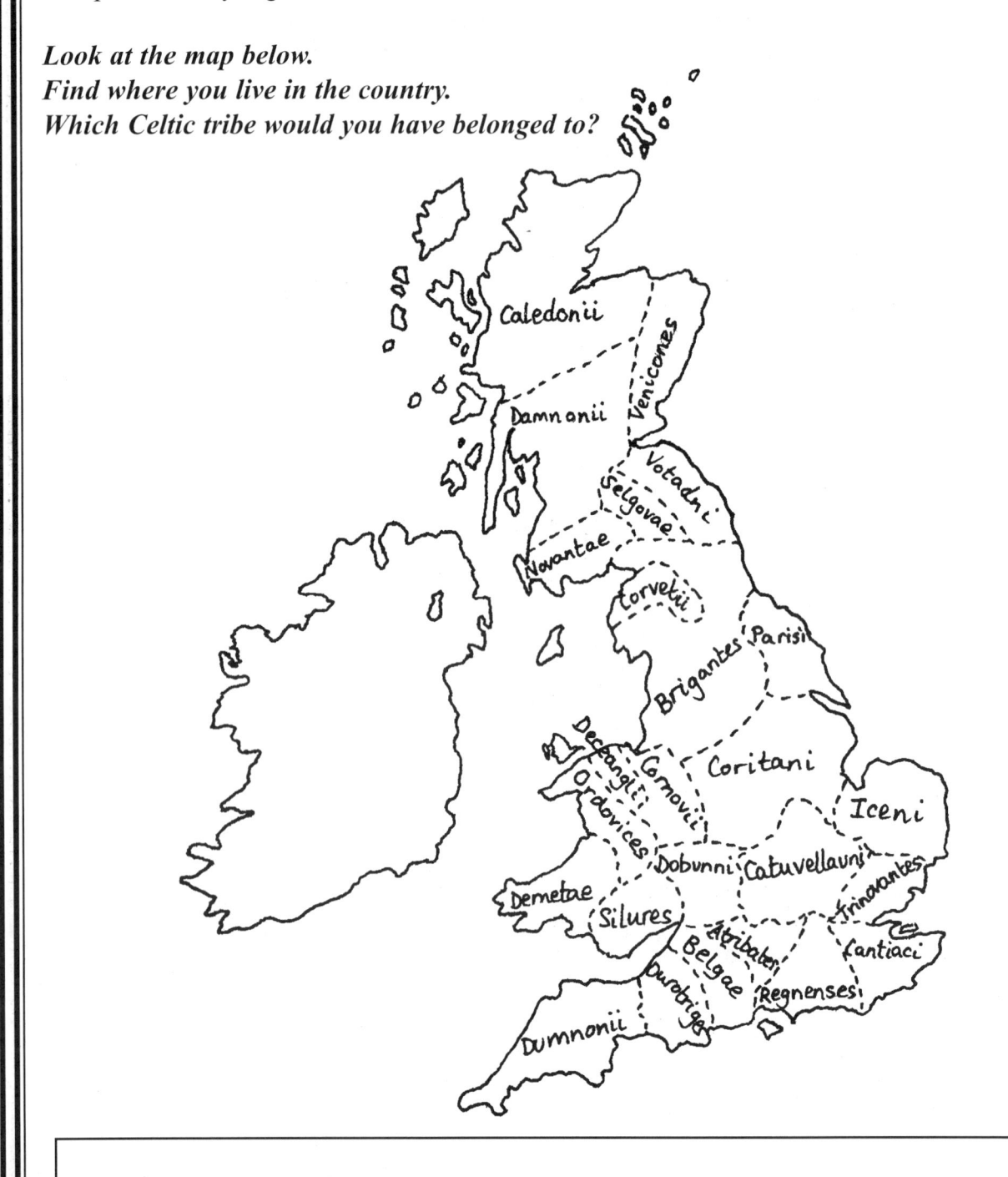

Look at the map below.
Find where you live in the country.
Which Celtic tribe would you have belonged to?

I would have belonged to the _____ tribe.

Celtic Britain II – A Mini Study

Religion

Religion was very important to the Celts. They were very superstitious people and worshipped about 400 gods. They did not think that the gods were friendly and sacrifices of animals and humans had to be made in order to please them.

They worshipped in woodland groves, beside rivers and lakes and in temples. Mistletoe and oak trees were sacred.

The Druids were Celtic religious leaders. They were 'priests' who performed the ceremonies, sacrificed animals and encouraged the Celts to fight fiercely. They could foretell the future too. The Celts buried dead people with objects, which they thought they might need in the afterlife. The Celts believed that a person's soul was in the head, so they collected the heads of their enemies as battle trophies!

Find out about the Roman religion.

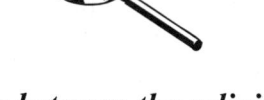

Make a list of the similarities and differences between the religion of the Celts and the Romans.

Religion of the Celts	Religion of the Romans

Celtic Britain III – A Mini Study

Festivals

The Celts had a number of farming festivals. *Illustrate them below:*

Celtic Festivals

Imbolc: - was celebrated on February 1st. This was when the ewes produced milk.

Beltane 'good fire': - was celebrated on May 1st and was when the cattle were put out to graze. They had to walk through the smoke and flames of bonfires in order to purify them.

Lughnasa: - was the harvest festival on August 1st when crops were gathered, such as peas, beans, rye, oats, wheat and barley.

Samain: - was celebrated from October 31st to November 1st and was the Celtic New Year. Spare animals were killed and eaten. The spirit world was important and the celebrations were a little like our Hallowe'en.

Celtic Britain IV – A Mini Study

Clothes

The Celts wore bright and colourful clothes made of wool and linen with striped and checked patterns. The women wore long dresses and men wore tunics and trousers with woollen cloaks. They wove all their woollen clothing. They wore very decorative jewellery such as belts, buckles and brooches. Men had long moustaches but no beards. The women wore their hair long and made their own make-up from berries and herbs, which they grew. Their shoes were made from leather.

How to make a Celtic Brooch

Look at different Celtic Designs. Decide what shape your brooch will be and make this out of card.

Create your own Celtic design using a medium-thick string, by twisting it. When you are happy with your string design, carefully glue this onto the card brooch.

Cover the card carefully with tin foil and smooth over without ripping it. The pattern should show through the foil.

Dyeing

The Celts dyed wool and could make many different shades and colours. They used leaves and berries from brambles, nettles and dock. They would then heat these and add the wool for dyeing. Before this, the wool was soaked in stale urine!

Celtic Britain V – A Mini Study

Women

Celtic women were respected and sometimes became rulers. This would mean that they would make decisions about the tribe, meet with the Druids and lead the tribe into battle. Boudicca was the most famous female tribe leader. Women looked after their own property, decided whom they should marry and worked outside the home. Women ground corn to make flour and brewed ale to drink. They cooked meat and dyed cloth which they wove.

Roman women could not decide whom they could marry. This was the decision of the woman's father. When she did get married, a Roman woman's husband looked after her property. She stayed at home to look after her children and did not work outside the home unless she was poor. Only men held positions of power. A woman was not equal to a man.

Write down the differences and similarities between Celtic and Roman women.

Differences	Similarities

Celtic Britain VI - A Mini Study

Produce

The Celts were very skilled people and many Celtic people became very rich from trading their goods.

__Illustrate and label the following products that the Celts produced:__

They made their own weapons, horseshoes, cooking pots and farming tools:

They decorated swords, shields, horse harnesses with bronze and made ornate jewellery such as brooches:

They also grew their own crops including wheat, barley, beans, turnips and parsnips:

They kept a number of animals, such as cows, pigs, goats and sheep, to give them meat, milk, leather and wool:

Celtic Britain VII – A Mini Study

How to make a Celtic Pot

You will need:

**CLAY
A FLAT STICK**

Roll out long sausages of clay and join the ends carefully. Coil them around in a spiral to make the shape of a bowl or a pot.

Smooth the pot inside and outside with the stick until the joins have disappeared. You may like to carve some patterns in the clay using a stick. Leave in the sun to harden, fire in a kiln or bake in an oven.

Celtic Britain VIII – A Mini Study

Warfare

The Celts were aggressive people and the warriors were the most important members of the tribe. They built hill forts to protect themselves. They had bronze and iron weapons (spears and long shields) which were beautifully decorated with patterns. They often rode in chariots, which were decorated with bronze and iron and were pulled by horses. They did not fight in chariots but fought on foot. They wore helmets decorated with bronze but they did not wear any body armour, only their normal clothes. A warrior's hair was stiff and pale because they rubbed chalk on to it when it was wet. Warriors used a blue dye (from woad plant) to paint and tattoo their bodies and faces.

Draw a Celtic Warrior

> They drive about in chariots, throw their weapons and generally break the ranks of the enemy with the very dread of their horses and noise of their wheels.
>
> **(Caesar 4.33)**

> Come, Romans. It is better for us to die manfully than to be captured and impaled, to see our own entrails cut from us. Let us conquer them or die.
>
> **(Suetonius)**

What do Suetonius and Caesar both think about the Celtic warriors in Britain?

Celtic Britain IX – A Mini Study

Celtic Houses

Ordinary Celtic people lived on farms. They lived in simple, circular, thatched houses, made mainly of branches and clay. A wooden fence or an earth bank and ditch separated the houses or group of houses. There was only one room in a typical house. In the centre was a fire and they hung meat above it. Smoke from the fire preserved the meat and stopped it from rotting. They cooked in pots over this fire. Sometimes they had a clay oven where they could bake bread etc. They ate their food from wooden bowls, not at a table but sitting on the floor. Their beds were simple, usually just a pile of straw covered by rags. They had a wooden loom inside the house in order to weave their clothes. Outside their houses, their animals were kept in enclosures.

Read the description above and draw a plan of the inside of a Celtic house in the box below. Don't forget to label it.

A Celtic House

Celtic Britain X - A Mini Study

Celtic Houses

Celtic tribes (called Caledonians) also lived in Scotland. They were wild and warlike people. They lived in different types of houses: -

Crannog

Broch

Hill Fort

Earth House

Look at the pictures of each of the houses above and read the facts about them on the next page. Think of the disadvantages and advantages of living in each house. Write them in the boxes provided on the next page.

I would least like to live in a ………………………………… because:

Did you know?
The Romans called the Celts in Scotland the Picts or 'The Painted People' because the warriors painted their bodies before charging into battle.

Celtic Britain XI – A Mini Study

Broch
A Broch was not easy to capture. It was difficult to climb the walls because of the shape. Holes could not be knocked in it as the walls were so thick. The door was very small.

Advantages	Disadvantages

Hill Fort
A Hill Fort was built with ditches and banks to prevent attack from enemies. A lookout tower was built so that enemies could be spotted far off.

Advantages	Disadvantages

Crannog
In Scotland some Crannogs were built on lochs. This made them very difficult to attack, as the enemy would have to approach by boat. Sometimes they had underwater paths leading to them.

Advantages	Disadvantages

Earth House
An Earth House was safe as it was underground and not very visible.

Advantages	Disadvantages

Celtic Britain XII – A Mini Study

Write an advertisement for a Celtic Round House, a Broch, a Crannog or an Earth House as if it was for sale during Celtic times.

Read these modern examples of advertisements to help you with the style.

FOR SALE

Beautiful, light, detached, modern house in excellent condition, near to centre of town. Attractive brick front. Large kitchen/diner, sitting room with doors into south facing garden, 3 bedrooms and 2 bathrooms. Must be viewed.

Contact M. Ovehouse & Sons

DETACHED COUNTRY COTTAGE

For sale: A picturesque cottage dating from 18th Century, with a wealth of exposed timbers and spacious accommodation.

Recently modernised with central heating. Approx. 2 miles from the nearest village.

- Hall, drawing room, dining room, study, conservatory, fitted kitchen
- Utility room, shower room
- 4 bedrooms, bathroom
- Partial double glazing, wood flooring, and some carpets
- Good sized gardens
- Garage and shed
- 5 acres of land

Interested purchasers should contact R.E. Movals as soon as possible.

TOWN FLAT FOR SALE

Georgian first floor one bedroom flat for sale in town centre. Period features include cornices, open fireplace, original stone-flagged floor, working shutters and sash windows. Shared garden/drying green. The property is in need of some renovation although outside stonework is in good condition. Hall, lounge, kitchen/dining room, bedroom, bathroom with cast iron bath, good storage.

Offers to S.U.R. Veyor Ltd. by the end of the month

You will have to be careful to include all the features of Celtic houses and remember not to have central heating and garages! Don't forget to include a picture too.

Idea
Put all the advertisements together to make a property section of a Celtic Newspaper.

Celtic Britain XIII – A Mini Study

PROPERTY ADVERTISEMENT PAGE

For Sale

THE ROMAN ARMY I
WEIGHTS AND EQUIPMENT

A ROMAN LEGIONARY SOLDIER

Label the soldier's equipment in Latin and English in the correct box and match it to the picture. The 'ROMAN ARMY SHEET II' will help you.

Colour the picture

THE ROMAN ARMY II

WEAPONS AND EQUIPMENT

Soldiers' weapons and armour:

1. **Short sword**	gladius	*for stabbing and cutting victims. If used with force, it could break a victim's body armour.*
2. **Iron dagger**	pugio	*for stabbing.*
3. **Javelin**	pilum	*had sharp iron points. When it was thrown at the shield of the enemy, it bent, making it difficult to pull out. This would trip up the enemy who would then have to throw his shield away, unable to free himself. The Roman soldier would then attack with his gladius.*
4. **Metal armour/belt**	lorica segmentata / balteus	*were made from metal strips.*
5. **Bronze helmet**	galea	*which protected the head and the back of the neck. It was made of metal and was decorated.*
6. **Curved metal shield**	scutum	*was made of wood, bronze and leather. It was painted red, brown, and beige. It was curved to protect the body, was light to carry and had a strap on the reverse so that it could be hung over the shoulder during marches.*
7. **Standard**	aquila	*usually had an eagle on it. Other standards were used and had the portrait of the emperor or the name and number of the legion.*
8. **Tunics**	cingulum	*were made of wool, leather or linen and were red.*
9. **Sandals**	caliga	*were made of leather. The thick soles had hobnails to make them last longer.*

THE ROMAN ARMY III
LONG-RANGE WEAPONS

The following long-range weapons were used by the Romans:

Catapult   •   Mangonel or Onager   •   Ballista

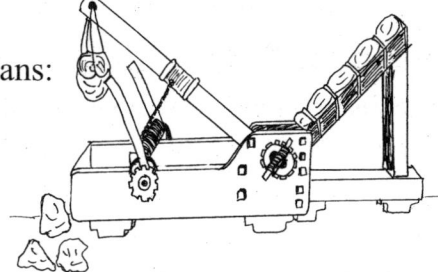

FIND OUT . . . *In groups, find out about one of these weapons, what it did and how successful it was. Try to make a model of one out of lollipop sticks and dowels.*
The Roman Army Technology Sheet III may help you with your design.

An Onager was able to hurl a heavy missile about 180 metres.

Work out how far this is, in your playground or a field. Compare this distance with throwing a ball by hand. How far can you throw the ball and what is the difference between your throw and that of the Onager?

TEST	ONAGER	DISTANCE OF BALL THROW	DIFFERENCE
1	180 m		
2	180 m		
3	180 m		

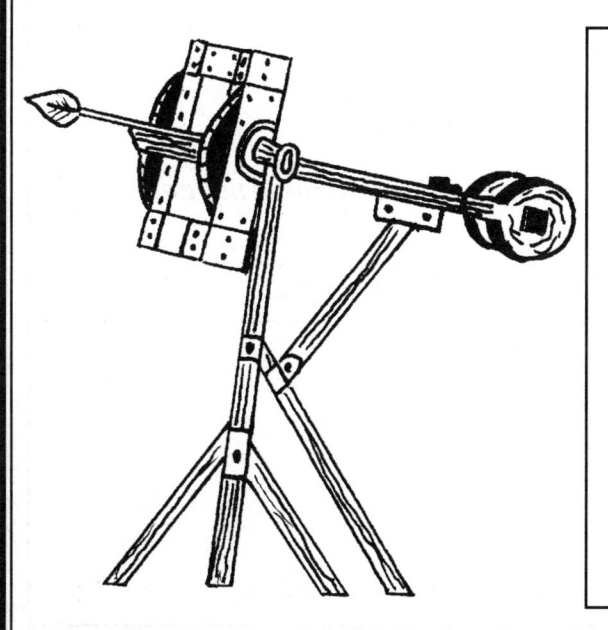

Did you know?

In A.D. 184, a Roman General showered an enemy ship with pottery jars, using a catapult. The jars contained poisonous snakes, which were freed on the smashing of the jars! He caused great confusion and this contributed to the victory of this General.

The Romans were also known to hurl the dead bodies of their enemies and animals over the enemy's walls to cause disease.

THE ROMAN ARMY IV

ORGANISATION OF THE ARMY

The Roman Empire was very powerful because of the size of its army. There were about 500,000 men who served and kept order.

The army was divided into **LEGIONS (legiones)** of foot soldiers. Each legion had about 5 - 6,000 soldiers and they had their own eagle standard **(aquila)**, which they carried into battle. The standard bearer was very important and he had to protect the standard. He wore a bear or lion skin. The legionaries were the best soldiers and were expected to serve in the army for around 25 years.

The legion was divided into ten groups, called **COHORTS**. Each Cohort was divided into six **CENTURIES**. (One century was made up of about 80 men). The cohort was easy to move on a battlefield. Usually it was arranged in 3 lines:

FRONT

| 4 COHORTS |
| 3 COHORTS |
| 3 COHORTS |

There were also **AUXILIARIES** in the Roman army who had specialised skills and were trained cavalrymen, archers and slingers. They were also organised into cohorts. Auxiliaries were not usually Roman Citizens until they left the army.

The Roman army had an enormous number of troops. They had gleaming armour and arms. They marched in orderly columns behind their standard bearers. They were always extremely well organised in their marches and on the battlefield.

What impression do you think the Celts had when they first saw the Roman army?

Write down the main differences and similarities between the Roman army and the Celtic warriors in the table below:

ROMANS	CELTS

ROMAN ARMY V

ORGANISATION OF THE ARMY - FIGHTING MEN

Below are a Roman Soldier and a Celtic Warrior.
Colour them in and then answer the questions at the bottom of the page.

Look at the clothing and equipment of each soldier.
How do they compare?

Which would you rather be - a Celtic warrior or a Roman soldier? Give reasons for your choice:

ROMAN ARMY VI
ARMY RESEARCH

GROUP RESEARCH

In groups, find out about the Roman Army.
Use the following questions and think of others to help you.
You may like to display your work or give a presentation.

Read the sheet *'Life as a Roman Soldier'* for some more information for your research.

Could anyone join the army?

Could soldiers get married while they were in the army?

How long did soldiers stay in the army?

What did a centurion do?

Who was in charge?

Who were the legionaries?

What was the food like?

What was a Roman fort like?

EXTRA
Make a poster to attract and persuade people into joining the Roman army.
You could make a Roman version of the World War I poster and in it state the good things about the army.

ROMAN ARMY VII
LIFE AS A ROMAN SOLDIER

Imagine that you are a Roman Soldier getting ready to leave on a campaign in Britain. You may be away for some years, including during the winter.

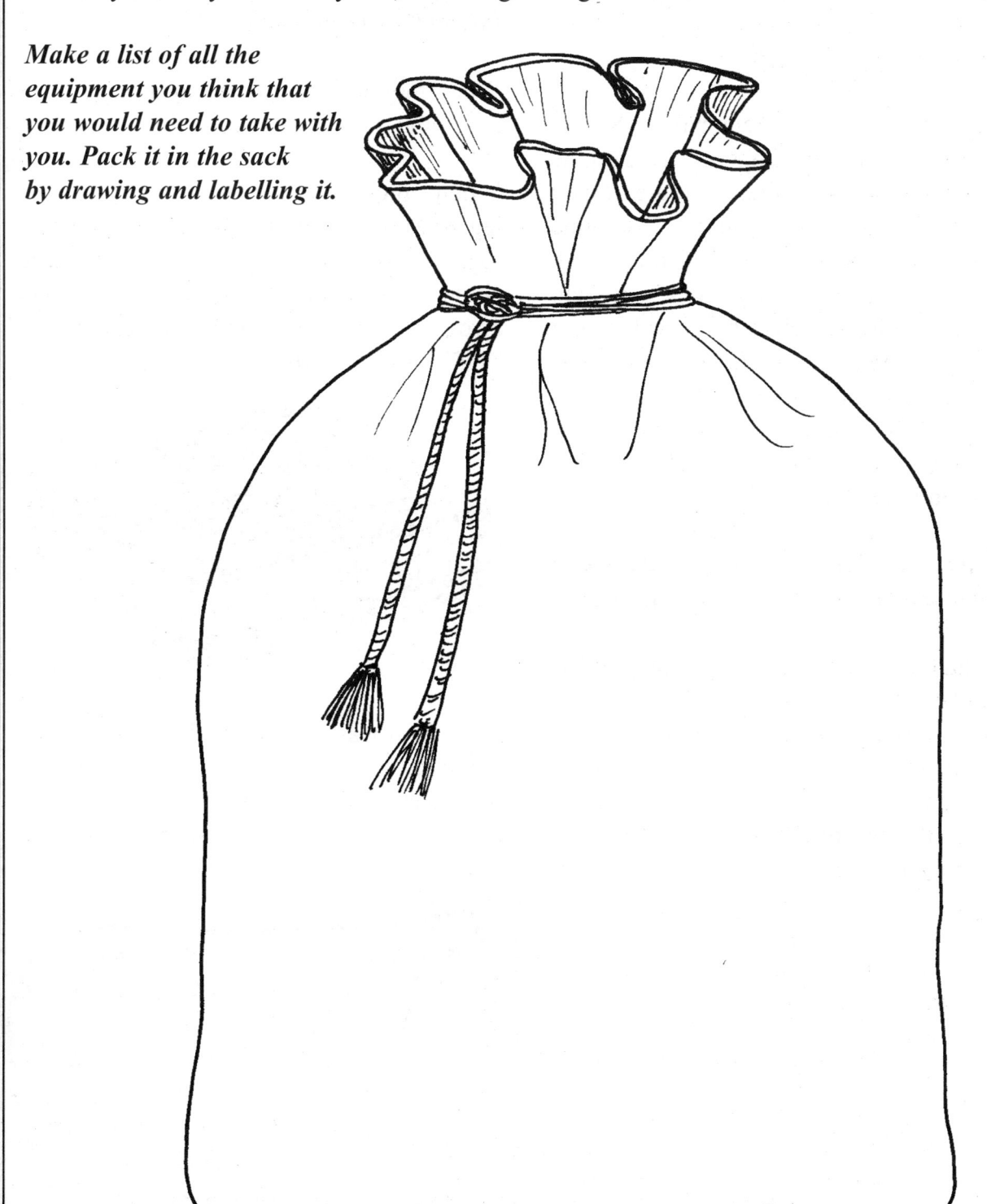

Make a list of all the equipment you think that you would need to take with you. Pack it in the sack by drawing and labelling it.

Now compare your answers with the kit that the soldiers took with them as described in the Roman Army Sheet VIII.

ROMAN ARMY VIII

LIFE AS A ROMAN SOLDIER

What was life like in the Roman army?

Was it easy or tough?

Roman soldiers, called legionaries, had to be strong and fit. The Emperor relied on the army to defend his empire. A soldier joined the army for about 20-25 years. Discipline was very strict and they had to train hard. They were trained to ride horses, march, swim, and fight, as well as build bridges and roads. They marched about 20 miles a day, carrying their equipment and wearing their armour. Their shields and swords were sometimes heavier than the real ones that they used in battle.

Why do you think the Roman soldiers had heavier shields and swords for training?

They had to wear a cloak which they used as a blanket at night, as well as carry their food, a cooking pot, digging tools, an axe, two sharp stakes, clothes and their camping equipment. They were expected to build a camp at the end of the day's march. They made trenches and banks around the camp to defend their tents when they were in enemy country and learned to do this very fast and under pressure.

When they needed to stay in a place for a long time, they built a stone fort.

When they marched into battle, the legionaries sometimes held their shields together to make a wall, and lifted these above their heads to protect them from arrows. This formation was called the TORTOISE or **testudo.**

If a soldier was in the army, he might not see his family for many years. The soldiers were paid well and they were given land to build a villa when they retired from the army.

Write a soldier's handbook using the information above.

You may want to include sections on the following:

- Selection
- Training
- Equipment
- Service
- Any other information a soldier may need to know.

A soldier . . . should have alert eyes and should hold up his head. He should be broadchested with powerful shoulders and muscular arms . . . he should not have a big stomach or a fat bottom. He should have muscular calves and feet. If he has these features it doesn't matter if he is a little short. It is better to be strong than tall.

VEGETIUS *(a Roman official)*
4th Century A.D.

THE ROMAN ARMY IX

BRITISH FORTS

The Roman Army had three fort bases in Britain: at Caerleon, York and Chester. Other important military places were Gloucester and Lincoln. They did not stay long in Scotland and never invaded Ireland. The British province of the Roman Empire only included England and Wales.

1. *Label Scotland, Wales, Caerleon, York, Chester, Gloucester, Lincoln and London on the map below.*
2. *Label Hadrian's Wall and the Antonine Wall.*
3. *Shade in the whole Roman province of Britain in colour.*

ROMAN ARMY X
TECHNOLOGY I

1. Design a Military Standard

Roman legions had their own standards. They were carried into battle and were a symbol of the legion. An aquila had an eagle on it. Others had the portrait of the Emperor, laurel leaves, or the name and number of the legion.

What you need:
- a thick stick like a broom handle
- stiff card or cardboard
- scissors
- paper plates
- paints
- sellotape

What to do:
(i) Cut a rectangle from the card and paint it and the paper plates with Roman-looking designs.
(ii) Attach the plates and card onto the handle to finish your standard.

2. Make a Roman Soldier

What you need:
- soldier template (separate sheet)
- card
- scissors
- coloured paper
- shiny paper or foil
- pens
- split pins

What to do:
(i) Cut out the template on the next page with scissors.
(ii) Mount the pieces carefully on to card and cut out again.
(iii) Now decorate your Roman soldier using coloured and shiny paper. Draw on his face using your pens.
(iv) Put the soldier together using split pins so that his arms and legs move.
(v) Make him a sword and a shield.

ROMAN ARMY XI

TECHNOLOGY II

Template for a Roman Soldier:

ROMAN ARMY XII

TECHNOLOGY III

How to make a simple model ballista:

What you need:
- wooden spatulas
- 1cm thick wooden dowelling (rectangular)
- thin sticks or round dowelling
- small / medium elastic band
- wood glue and sellotape
- small nails, hammer, saw, sandpaper

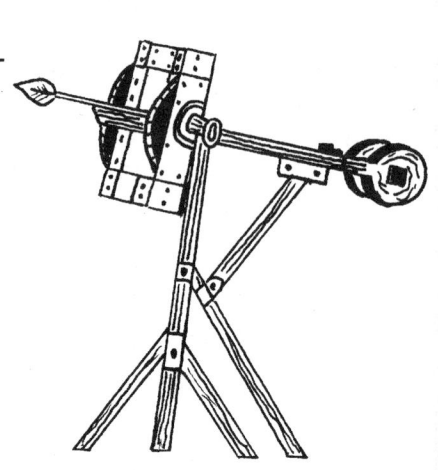

What to do:
- (i) Cut two wooden spatulas to a length of 15cm.
- (ii) Saw the rectangular dowelling to two lengths. One of 16cm and the other 10cm.
- (iii) Sand the ends of the cut wood.
- (iv) Hammer the spatulas (using small nails) on to both sides of one end of the 16cm piece of wooden dowelling, so that they are nailed at an angle *(see illustration below)*.
- (v) Glue the smaller length of rectangular dowelling on top of the larger length.
- (vi) Cut the thin round dowelling into a length of 10cm. Cut the elastic band so it is one length.
- (vii) Using sellotape, attach the elastic band to each end of one of the small thin sticks. Glue this stick (but not the band) across the top of the smaller wooden block.
- (viii) Use the other thin sticks of wood as arrows.
- (ix) When completely dry, fire your arrows by pulling them back using the elastic band and see how far they fly!

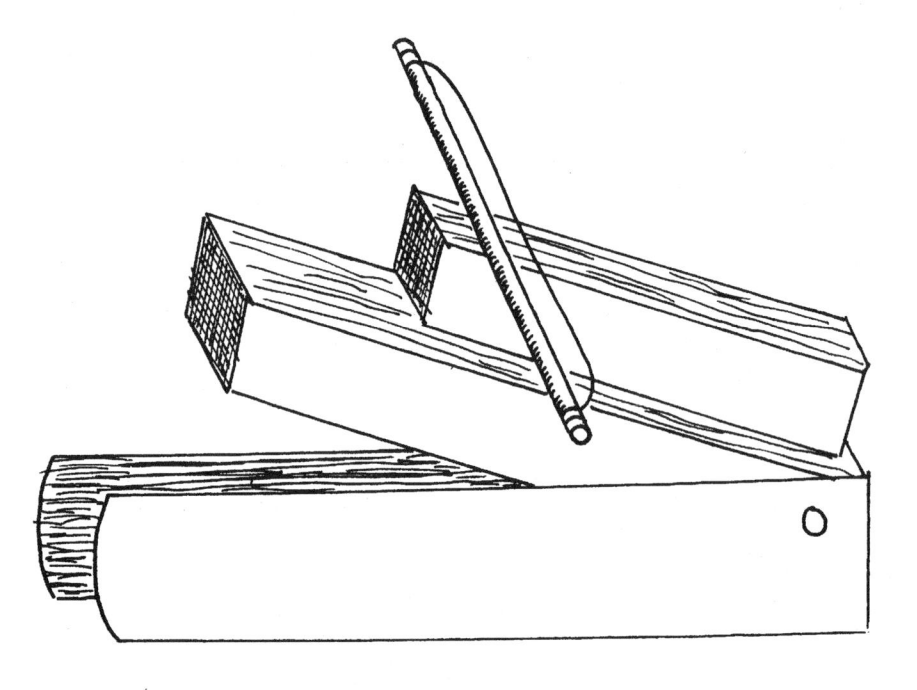

WHY DID JULIUS CAESAR INVADE BRITAIN IN 55 B.C.?

Read the primary sources and information below.

Julius Caesar conquered Gaul (France) in 55 B.C. It was a fierce battle against the Gauls who had been helped by their neighbours the Britons. Julius Caesar was the first Roman general to decide to attack Britain because he claimed that he wanted to *teach its people a lesson,* for supporting the Gauls against him.

Caesar attempted to invade Britain twice. His first invasion in 55 B.C. was not successful due to the weather and the British warriors. He states:

> *They drive about in all directions in their chariots, throw their weapons and generally break the ranks of the enemy with the very dread of their horses and the noise of their wheels. They train and practise each day, becoming so skilful that they can even control their horses at full gallop on a steep hill and they can stop them straight away. They can run along the chariot pole, stand on the yoke and jump into the chariot as quick as lightning.*
>
> (Caesar IV.33)

Despite the fact that the first invasion of Britain in the end was not successful and his army had to withdraw, Caesar was proud that he had conducted an expedition anyway. The passage below, written by Caesar himself, describes his army's first dramatic landing in Britain and the Romans' initial success. However, things did not continue to be successful. Despite this, according to Cassius Dio, the Romans celebrated Caesar's first invasion for twenty days, inspired with the thought of future victory and another invasion of Britain.

> *The Romans had problems when they arrived in Britain and the natives frightened them. Their heavy armour weighed them down but they had to jump out of their ships to get ashore and fight them. They were not used to fighting in these conditions. The enemy threw their spears and their horsemen charged. Caesar lined up all the ships towards the enemy and they fired arrows, slings and catapults at them. One Roman soldier from the 10th legion, who carried the sacred eagle standard, prayed to the gods for victory. He led the soldiers towards the enemy. It was a hard battle but the Romans formed a battle line, charged and the enemy ran away.*
>
> (Caesar's Gallic War IV.24-26)

1. Why did Julius Caesar invade Britain? Was it a successful invasion in the end?

2. What difficulties did Julius Caesar face on his arrival in Britain?

3. Why might Julius Caesar have made his difficulties seem worse than they really were?

4. On the back of this sheet, draw and label all the different weapons that the Romans and Britons used that are mentioned by Caesar.

JULIUS CAESAR'S
SECOND INVASION OF BRITAIN - 54 B.C.

Caesar's second invasion of Britain in 54 B.C. was with a much larger army of twenty-seven thousand troops. He defeated the British King Cassivellaunus, ruler of the Catuvellauni tribe. Caesar therefore controlled the southeast of Britain and made it a part of the Roman Empire. He had to return to Gaul however, as there were uprisings there, leaving no Roman troops behind.

Caesar wrote some interesting comments about the natives of Britain:

> *They live on milk and flesh and wear skins. All the Britons paint themselves with woad, which gives their skin a bluish colour and makes them look very dreadful in battle. They wear their hair long and shave all their body except their head and upper lip. They have ten and even twelve wives each.*
>
> (Caesar's Gallic Wars V.14)

Suetonius claims that Caesar came to Britain because he hoped to get pearls and he was an enthusiastic collector of gems. He liked to compare their size by weighing them in his own hand.

Find out more about Julius Caesar

People thought about Julius Caesar in different ways. Some believed that he was selfish and very cruel and others liked him.

Ask your teacher for the Julius Caesar Planning Sheet to help you make some notes.

Find out and write as much as you can about Julius Caesar's life.

Was he good or bad (or both)?

Give reasons for your answer.

JULIUS CAESAR PLANNING PAGE

NOTES:

Early Life -

Military Life -

Political Career -

Popularity -

Death -

Find out what changes Julius Caesar made to the calendar and to Roman coins.

CLAUDIUS' INVASION OF BRITAIN

THE ROMAN TIMES A.D. 43

EMPEROR INVADES BRITAIN

EMPEROR CLAUDIUS SENT AN ARMY TO INVADE THE PROVINCE OF BRITAIN EARLIER THIS YEAR. NO ONE HAS ATTEMPTED THIS SINCE JULIUS CAESAR HIMSELF. CLAUDIUS' ARMY TERRIFIED THE LOCALS AND THE ROMAN ARMY HAS SETTLED.

WHY DID CLAUDIUS INVADE BRITAIN?

Since Julius Caesar's invasions, Britain was trading with the Romans. The Romans traded silver, cloth and wine but were attracted by the British tin and lead mines.

Emperor Claudius was becoming unpopular in Rome and he needed the citizens of Rome to support him to stay in power.

The army were becoming restless too, as the Empire was peaceful. Claudius was afraid that the army would turn against him, so he decided to attack Britain.

Above all, the invasion would boost his personal image and make him successful.

Claudius made three landings with four legions. He successfully defeated some tribes while others surrendered. He conquered much of the south of England. Some of the tribes rebelled against the Roman rule but others made peace.

Claudius and his troops were able to overcome eleven tribes successfully and establish Roman rule in Britain for the first time. The Romans celebrated this splendid triumph on his return to Rome. Roman soldiers remained in Britain.

1. *Do you think that Claudius was right to order an invasion so that he could seek popularity for himself? Say why.*

2. *Was Claudius successful in his invasion? Did it make him popular?*

CLAUDIUS' INVASION OF BRITAIN

Below are a number of reasons for Claudius wanting to invade Britain.

Cut out and arrange the following statements in order, starting with the most important. Stick them into your book or on to a piece of paper. Explain why you have put them in this order. You may like to discuss them with some friends first.

Claudius wanted to use the tin and lead produced in Britain.

Claudius wanted to expand the Roman Empire.

Claudius wanted to keep the Roman army from attacking him.

Claudius needed popularity and the support of the people of Rome.

The army was restless and needed a battle.

Claudius wanted to show everyone, including the British, that he was in control.

BOUDICCA I - THE WARRIOR QUEEN

INFORMATION PAGE

The Romans continued to defeat the British tribes who tried to revolt against them.

Prasutagus, the Iceni tribe leader, had decided that in order to keep his power and stay in charge of his tribe, it was best to side with the Romans. However, when he died, the Romans seized all of his property.

They treated his wife Boudicca and her daughters with cruelty.

In 61 A.D. Boudicca made a great speech, as recorded by Cassius Dio:

You all know the difference between slavery and freedom. Since the Romans came to Britain, we have been their slaves. They have taken all our possessions and we have to pay them taxes. We work on the land for them. I would rather die than pay taxes to them. It is our fault, as we allowed them to come to Britain and settle. We should have chased them away, as we once did with Julius Caesar. It is not too late. We do not owe our future children slavery, but the same freedom that we can remember.

Do not fear the Romans. They are not braver or greater than us. We are used to war. This region is known to us and is our ally. To them it is hostile and unknown. Let us defeat them and trust in good fortune. They are hares and foxes trying to rule over dogs and wolves.

Boudicca wanted freedom, revenge for her treatment and to stop the Romans from dominating. As a result of this speech, the Iceni tribe rose up against the Romans, led by Boudicca. She became one of Rome's most dangerous enemies.

Boudicca waited until the Romans were away fighting tribes in Wales and her tribe, the Trinovantes, burned Colchester and London. They beheaded the townspeople of London and threw their heads into the River Thames. They destroyed St Albans, and killed the entire population of about seventy thousand. Tacitus, a Roman, stated: *The Britons could not wait to cut throats, hang, burn and crucify . . .*

SUETONIUS, the Roman governor of Britain, realised that he had to destroy the Iceni tribe if the Romans were to stay in Britain. He raised an army of ten thousand soldiers to fight the rebels. The Romans were well armed and were able to overcome the Celts easily.

Boudicca, so as not to be captured by the Romans, escaped to the woods where it is believed she took poison and died. Her body was never found.

In order to avoid the same thing happening again, the Romans appointed Julius Agricola as Roman governor of Britain.

BOUDICCA II

Using the Boudicca Sheet I, imagine that you are Boudicca.

Write her diary entries for each stage of her fight against the Romans. Use the plan below to help you.

You may like to write it up on tea-stained paper to make it look like an authentic piece of writing.

Diary Plan

Early life with the Romans, under the leadership of Boudicca's father.

Death of Prasutagus, her husband and the treatment of the Iceni tribe by the Romans.

Boudicca's feelings and description of her own speech.

The defeat of Colchester, London and St. Albans.

The Romans' attack and the final defeat.

Final thoughts before she dies.

BOUDICCA III - WHAT DID SHE LOOK LIKE?

Cassius Dio wrote a description of Boudicca.

Read it carefully and then draw a picture of the warrior queen.

> *She was very tall and looked terrifying. Her eyes were fierce and her voice was harsh. She had very long red hair that hung down to her hips. Around her neck, she wore a large gold necklace. She always wore a tunic of many colours, covered by a thick cloak, which was fastened with a brooch. She grasped a spear as she spoke.*
>
> Cassius Dio LXII

Did you know? - While Boudicca rode in her chariot, she would slice off her victims' heads with her sword!

BOUDICCA

HADRIAN'S WALL

In A.D. 122, the Emperor Hadrian ordered his soldiers to build a wall across northern England, from the Solway Firth to the River Tyne, to separate Roman Britain from the wilder tribes of the north. It was to keep the Scottish barbarians (Caledonians) out of the Empire. It was cold, lonely and dangerous work and life must have been hard as the soldiers were always at risk of attack from the north. Hadrian visited in person to encourage the loyalty of his troops.

The wall took about seven years to build. It was 76 miles long, 3 metres thick and about 4 metres high. It was built by about 8,500 men in the Roman army who were very skilled builders, surveyors, architects and stonemasons.

The wall had 80 milecastles, large forts and turrets or watchtowers built along it. A ditch on the north side of the wall was very deep and wide. Soldiers therefore guarded the edge of the Empire securely.

Did you know?
Hadrian's Wall was built using 4 million tons of stone; some of the wall still exists today.

Using the facts above to help you, make a guidebook about Hadrian's Wall.

You will need to do some research as well, and to find some pictures.

THE ANTONINE WALL

In A.D. 138, **ANTONINUS PIUS** succeeded Hadrian and extended the frontier further north. He built the Antonine Wall in Scotland (Caledonia) in A.D. 142.

It stretched about 40 miles from the Clyde to the Forth. It had a stone base and was built with turf bricks and wooden battlements. 19 forts lay along the wall. Milestones were also set up along the wall. One surviving milestone has a carving of the emperor placing a laurel (a symbol of honour) onto the legion's eagle standard. It took 3 legions of soldiers two years to build the wall across the narrowest part of Britain. For 20 years, the Romans held this wall, but the Picts continually attacked the wall until the Romans retreated back to Hadrian's Wall.

1. *Mark the walls of Hadrian and Antoninus in the correct place on the map.*

2. *Write down why you think the Romans built two walls across Scotland and England.*

3. *What do you think life was like for those living near to the walls?*

4. *The Romans built the walls for different reasons. Number these four statements in order of importance* (1 being most important, 4 being the least):

To stop expanding the empire.

To keep the soldiers busy

To stop the northern tribes from attacking

To show the Britons that the Romans were in charge

Compare and discuss them with someone else's answers.

HOW TO MAKE A FORT ON HADRIAN'S WALL
SHEET I

You will need Sheet I & four copies of Sheet II to make this Roman Fort. Follow the instructions carefully.

INSTRUCTIONS

(i) Cut out the walls and the turrets of the fort and the gateway. Glue them on to card and cut out again.

(ii) Paint the walls and turrets to look like stone, and leave them to dry.

(iii) Cut the tab slots carefully and score the folds using a ruler and a pair of scissors.

(iv) Fold the turret and fix together with glue along the tab. Do the same with all the turrets.

(v) When dry, attach the turrets to the four walls, slotting them together using the tab slots.

(vi) Attach the gateway along one of the walls, in the centre. Cut between the two doors and around the arched section so that they open.

ROMAN FORT GATEWAY

HOW TO MAKE A FORT ON HADRIAN'S WALL

SHEET II

WALLS AND TURRETS

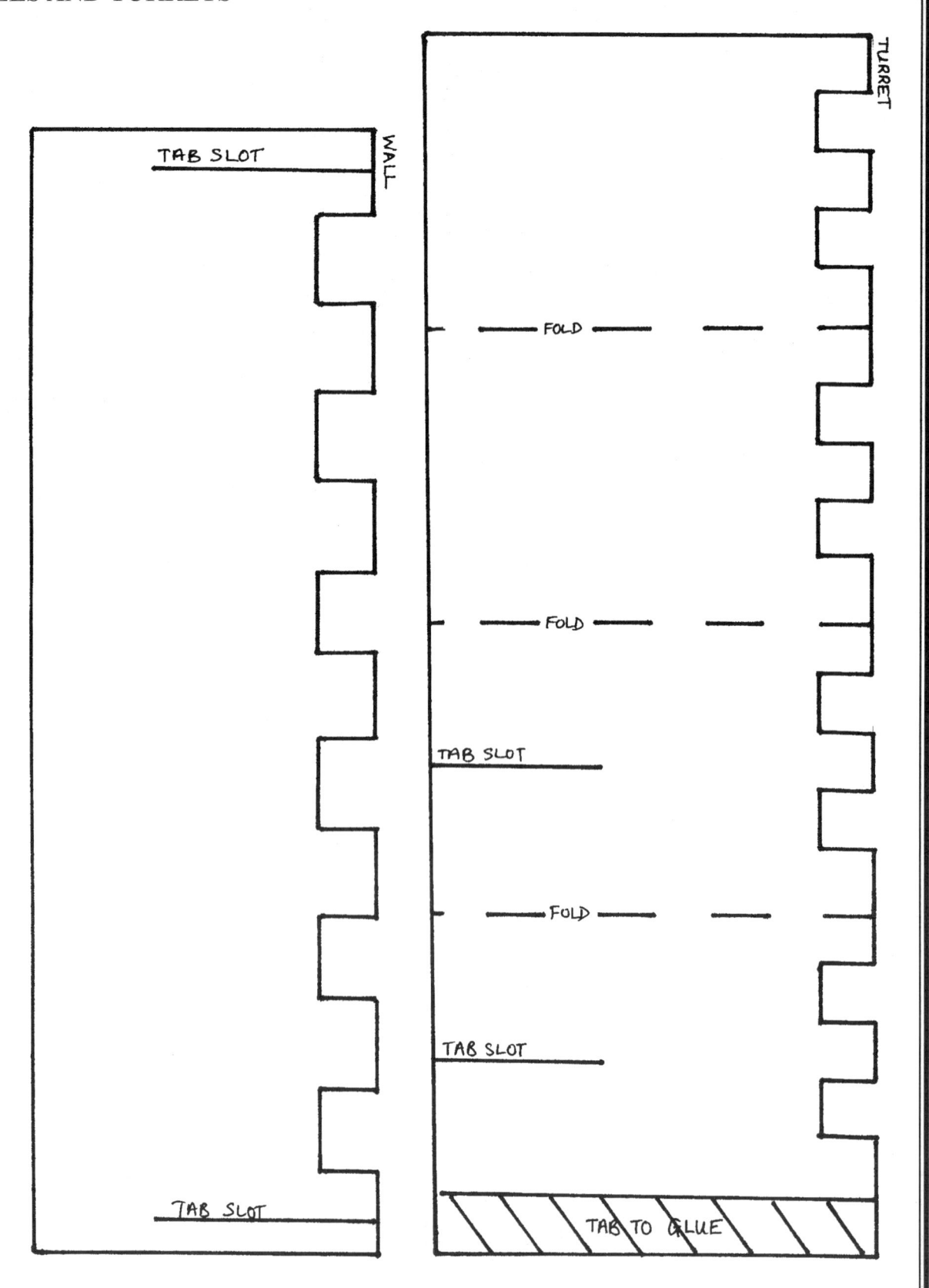

ROMAN BRITAIN TIMELINE

Make and illustrate a timeline showing the key events in Roman Britain as listed below:

55 B.C.	Julius Caesar lands at Dover. He wins some battles but returns to Gaul.
54 B.C.	Julius Caesar returns and defeats a main British tribe in the southeast. The Britons start to pay an annual tribute.
A.D. 43	Emperor Claudius invades and conquers the southeast of Britain. He captures the capital of the Catuvellauni tribe (Colchester).
A.D. 43-51	The Roman army moves through Britain defeating local tribes.
A.D. 60 - 122	Roman rule continues for a further 62 years. Hostile tribes continue to be defeated, except for the Caledonian tribes and the Picts.
A.D. 60	The Iceni Tribe rebel, led by Boudicca. Her army destroys Colchester (Camulodunum), London (Londinium) and St Albans (Verulamium) before being defeated.
A.D. 61	King of Catuvellauni tribe flees west, raises an army against the Romans but is captured. Agricola becomes Roman Governor of Britain (A.D. 78).
A.D. 122 - 410	Peace in Roman Britain. Many roads and towns are built. Christianity begins to spread.
A.D. 122	Hadrian's Wall is completed. This kept the tribes of the north away from Roman Britain.
A.D. 142	The Antonine Wall is built. More roads and towns are built.
A.D. 410	The Romans leave Britain and Britons are told to defend themselves.

MAPS TO SHOW THE GROWTH OF ROMAN INVASION

Colour the maps to show the growth of Roman Invasions in Europe:

UNDER THE RULE OF JULIUS CAESAR

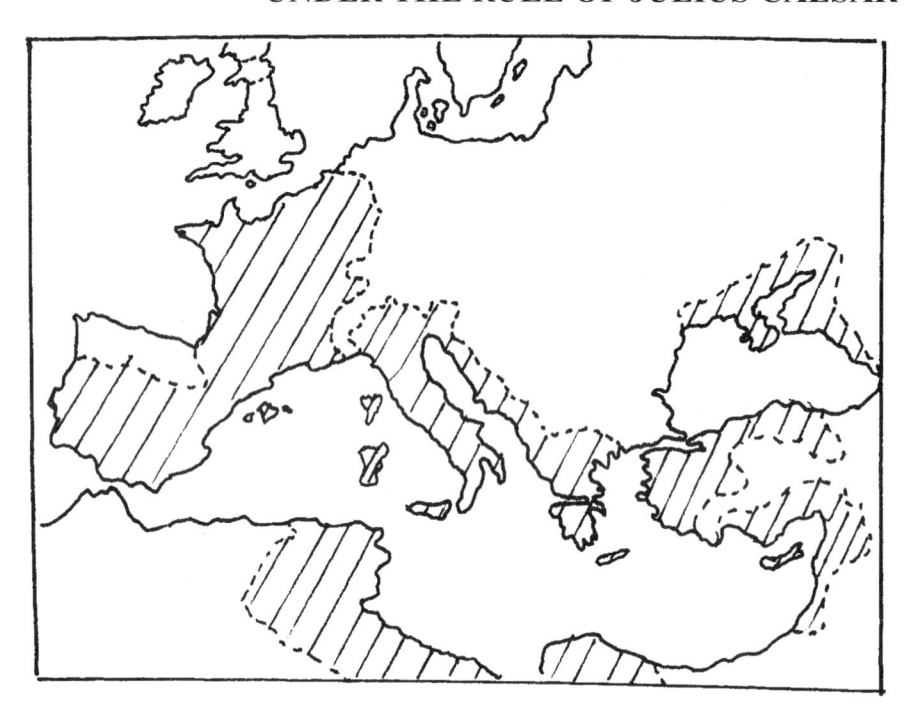

UNDER THE RULE OF EMPEROR HADRIAN

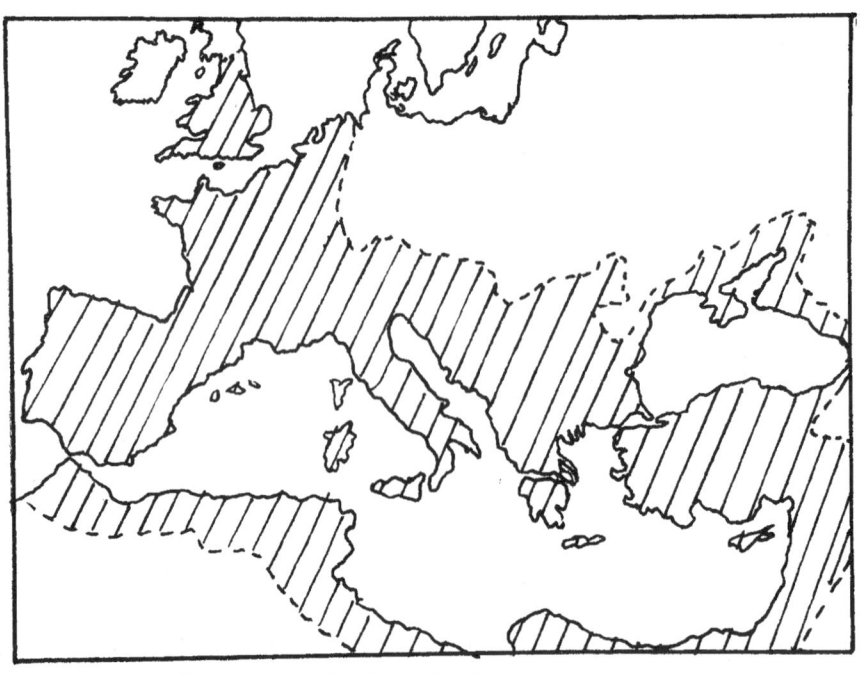

What do you notice about the Empire?

MAPS TO SHOW THE GROWTH OF ROMAN INVASION OF BRITAIN

Colour the maps to show the growth of Roman Invasions:

HADRIAN'S INVASION (A.D. 122)

ANTONINUS' INVASION (A.D. 142)

ROMAN ROADS I

Why do you think the Romans built roads? How did roads help these people below? Write down your reasons before reading the information below.

The Roman army built roads to allow people to move around easily. In Roman times, people travelled by horse and by cart or they walked. Supplies were carried quickly on roads. It was easier to trade using good roads, and soldiers needed to march across a country quickly. They needed proper roads, which were straight to allow easy and fast access.

Many of the roads that the Romans built connected between military forts. The network of roads helped to keep the country under control. Sometimes the Romans built an **agger**. This was a road on a raised bank, which allowed soldiers to see or impress the enemy.

Roman roads were built carefully and well. The bottom layer was made of large stones and was called the **statumen**. Above this was a layer of smaller stones called the **rudus**. Next was a layer of gravel called the **nucleus** and finally the top layer of large flat stones was called the **pavimentum**. They were designed to slope down from the middle to ditches that ran along the side of the road. The rain could therefore run off the road.

Roman roads could be up to 1 metre deep. All over the empire, minor roads were between 3-4.5 metres wide, and major roads could be about 7 metres wide. The roads of the Roman Empire stretched about 50,000 miles. Many remains of Roman roads still exist today.

Did you know?

ROMAN MAIL

The Emperor Augustus set up the **Cursus Publicus**. This was a postal system that the Romans used. Messengers rode on horseback on the roads, travelling in relays of about 30 miles. Letters were written on scrolls and fastened with a wax seal.

Communication was very important in such a large empire and the messengers had to travel at great speed.

ROMAN ROADS II

Read the information about Roman roads and answer these questions.

1. Why were good roads important to the Romans?

2. Who built the roads?

3. How do we know that a Roman road was built in layers?

4. What was the bottom layer of a road made of?

5. Why did the Romans build ditches on either side of a road?

6. What was an agger?

7. Label the cross-section of the road below using the Latin names and the English.

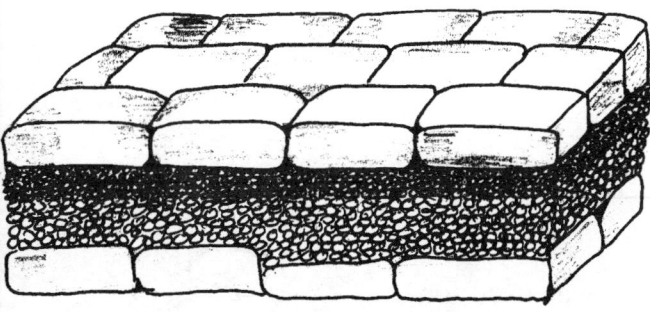

Cross-section of a Roman road

Milestones were placed along the roads, every Roman mile. This was about 1,500 metres or 1,000 paces (two steps per pace).

. . . an ideal Roman road is built in layers. VITRUVIUS

ROMAN ROADS III

Look at a good modern map of your local area of Britain.
Can you find any remains of Roman roads?
Some roads may still have their Roman names.
Which towns or cities do they run between?

Write your findings below:

Some names of towns in Britain come from Roman times.

Find some places with Latin names, like the ones in the box opposite.

See how many you can find, using your atlas.

> These place name **endings** come from the Latin word *castra*, which means 'a fort'.
> -chester   -cester   -caster
>
> These place names are found at the **beginning** of the word. They come from the time of the Romans and mean that there was a Roman road here.
> **Strat-**   **Street-**   **Stret-**
> **Streat-**   **Strad-**   **Sturt-**

Write them down below:

Eg.   Man**chester**   **Streat**ham

Extra:
Find out what an ODOMETER was and what it was used for.

ROMAN ROADS IV

Below is a map of the main Roman roads in Britain.

Carefully draw over the line of the following roads, using a different colour for each. Make a key and label it.

Fosse Way - running from Exeter to Lincoln.
Ermine Street - from London to Lincoln.
Watling Street - from Wroxeter to St Albans and Kent.

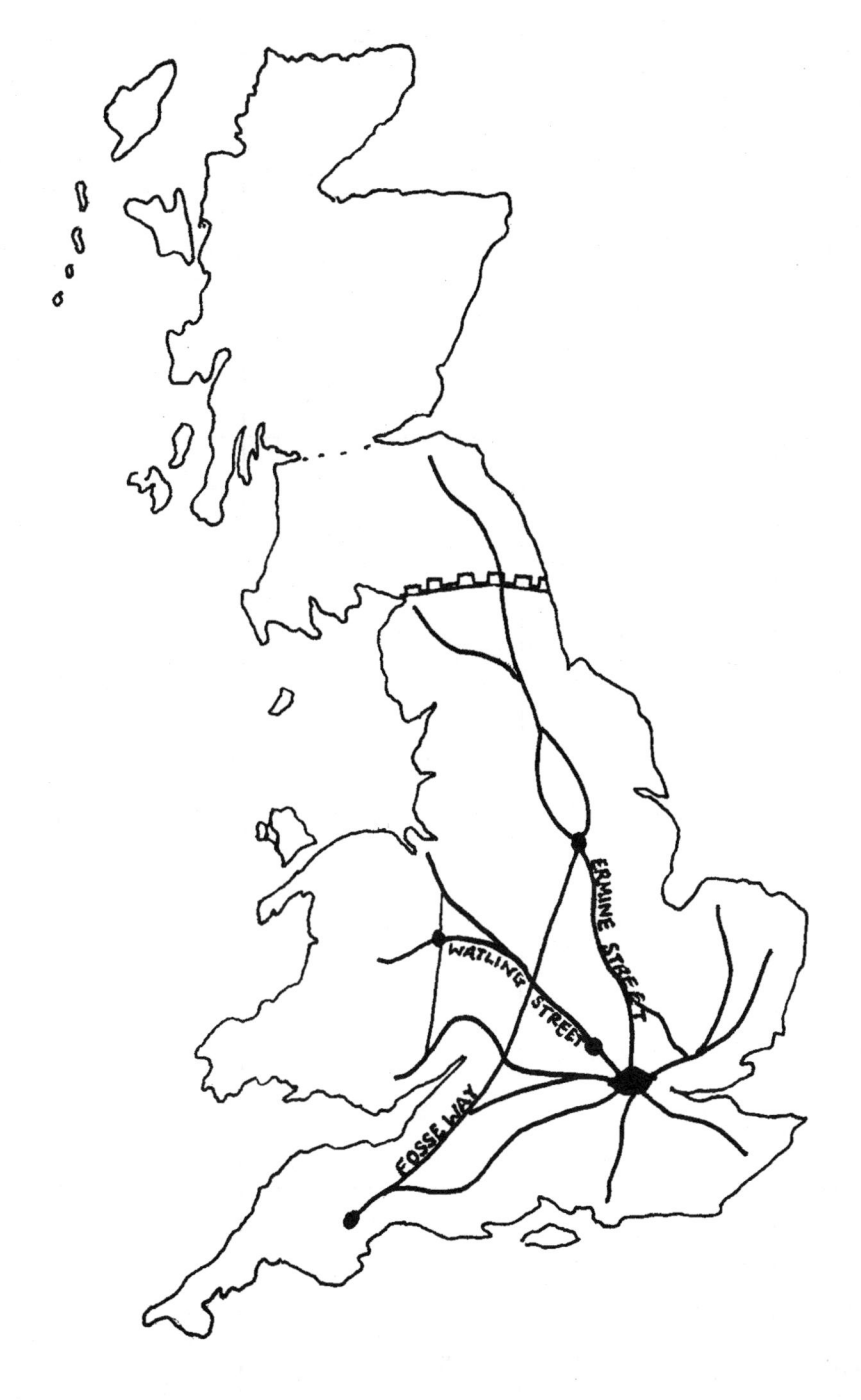

Look at a modern map of Britain.
Can you find these roads and are they still used today?

ROMAN ROADS V

You will need a modern road map of Britain and the Roman roads map.

Give the modern road names for these Roman roads and write down which towns or cities they lie between. Do the roads still exist or have they changed since Roman times?

Roman Road	Modern Roads	Towns	Changes
Watling Street			
Fosse Way			
Dere Street			
Ermine Street			

ROMAN TOWNS IN BRITAIN I

In Britain, the Romans built many towns. Many of our modern towns and cities are built on the same sites that the Romans chose.

1. Choose a Roman town like York, St Albans or Lincoln. Find it on a modern map of Britain.

2. Using the map, make a clear sketch map of the area below.

3. Draw on the town, any rivers or nearby seas. Make a key.

4. Using a good map or an Ordnance Survey map of the area, mark in any hills or mountains. Is the town built on a hill? You will need to look for contour lines.

5. Mark in any other geographical features (e.g. woods). Add them to your key.

6. What geographical reasons were there for the Romans to choose this site to build a town? Look at your map and answers above to help you.

SKETCH MAP

ROMAN TOWNS IN BRITAIN II

The Romans had Latin names for the towns in Roman Britain.

Look at the map labelled below with the Latin town names. Write down which towns these are today in the box at the bottom of the page.

Some you will find easy to identify. For others you may need to do some research or to use an atlas. Good luck!

	Roman Towns	Modern British Towns
1.	Eboracum	
2.	Deva	
3.	Viroconium Cornoviorum	
4.	Glevum	
5.	Isla Dumnoniorum	
6.	Lindum	
7.	Londinium	
8.	Durobrivae	
9.	Aquae Sulis	
10.	Verulamium	
11.	Corinium	
12.	Camulodunum	

ROMAN TOWNS IN BRITAIN III

The Romans built carefully planned, neat towns, using a grid pattern. Straight roads crossed at right angles.

Roman towns consisted of many different buildings. There were houses, shops and public buildings. The styles of architecture were very different from the round buildings of the Celts. The Romans built most buildings using wood, but some were built of stone or brick and tiles were also used on the roofs. Quite often, houses and shops were combined, where the shop faced on to the street and the house was behind.

In the centre of the town, at a major crossroad, was the forum. This was the heart of the town. Here there was usually a covered walk way or portico with columns. On one side of the forum was the town hall and law court. There were also offices, storerooms and market stalls here. The forum was the centre of the government and trade. You would find sellers of pottery, leather and glass, bakers, ironmongers, butchers and carpenters here also.

Other buildings found in Roman towns in Britain and all over the Empire were: bath houses, temples and shrines.

Did you know?
The Latin for town was **urbs**. Our word 'urban' comes from this word.

Did you know?
The Romans invented concrete.

ROMAN TOWNS IN BRITAIN IV

Below are some pictures. Cut them out and glue them carefully on the town grid. Use the co-ordinates to plot the correct place on the grid.

1. **AMPHITHEATRE**
   (3,13) (4,13) (5,13)
   (3,14) (4, 14) (5,14)
   (3,15) (4,15), (5,15)

2. **ARCH**
   (11,3) (11,4)

3. **CITY GATES**
   (1,9) (9,1) (9,17) (17,9)

4. **GRAVE STONES**
   (place these along the road outside city gate (1,9)

5. **BATHS**
   (11,13) (11,14) (11,15)
   (12,13) (12,14) (12,15)

6. **GYMNASIUM**
   (6,14) (7,14) (8,14)
   (6,15) (7,15) (8,15)

7. **AQUEDUCT**
   (13,15) (14,15) (16,15), (17,15) and beyond the city walls.

8. **TEMPLE TO JUPITER**   **TEMPLE TO APOLLO**
   (3,2) (4,2) (3,3) (4,3)   (14,12) (15,12) (14,13) (15,13)

9. **THEATRE**
   (5,10) (6,10) (7,10) (8,10)
   (5,11) (6,11) (7,11) (8,11)

10. **LIBRARY**
    (12,11)

11. **FORUM WALLS**
    (5,4) (5,5) (5,6) (5,7) (5,8) (6,8) (7,8) (8,4) (8,5) (8,6) (8,7) (8,8)
    BASILICA (Law Courts)
    (5,4) (6,4) (7,4) (8,4)

12. **DOMUS**
    (12,6) (12,7) (13,6) 13,7)

13. **FOUNTAIN** (place between these co-ordinates)
    (6,6) (7,6)

14. **BAR** (2,7)   **INN** (3,7)   **BAKERY** (3,6)

15. **INSULAE** (apartment blocks) (15,5) (15,6)

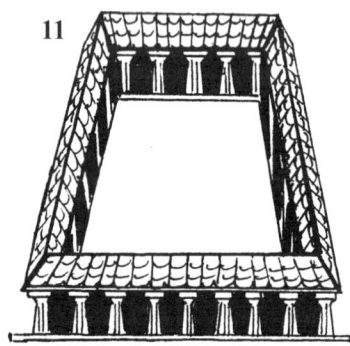

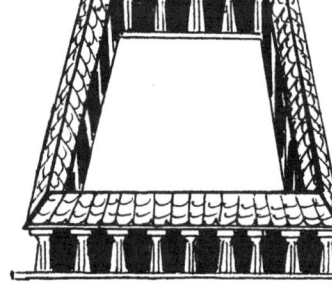

68

ROMAN TOWN PLAN

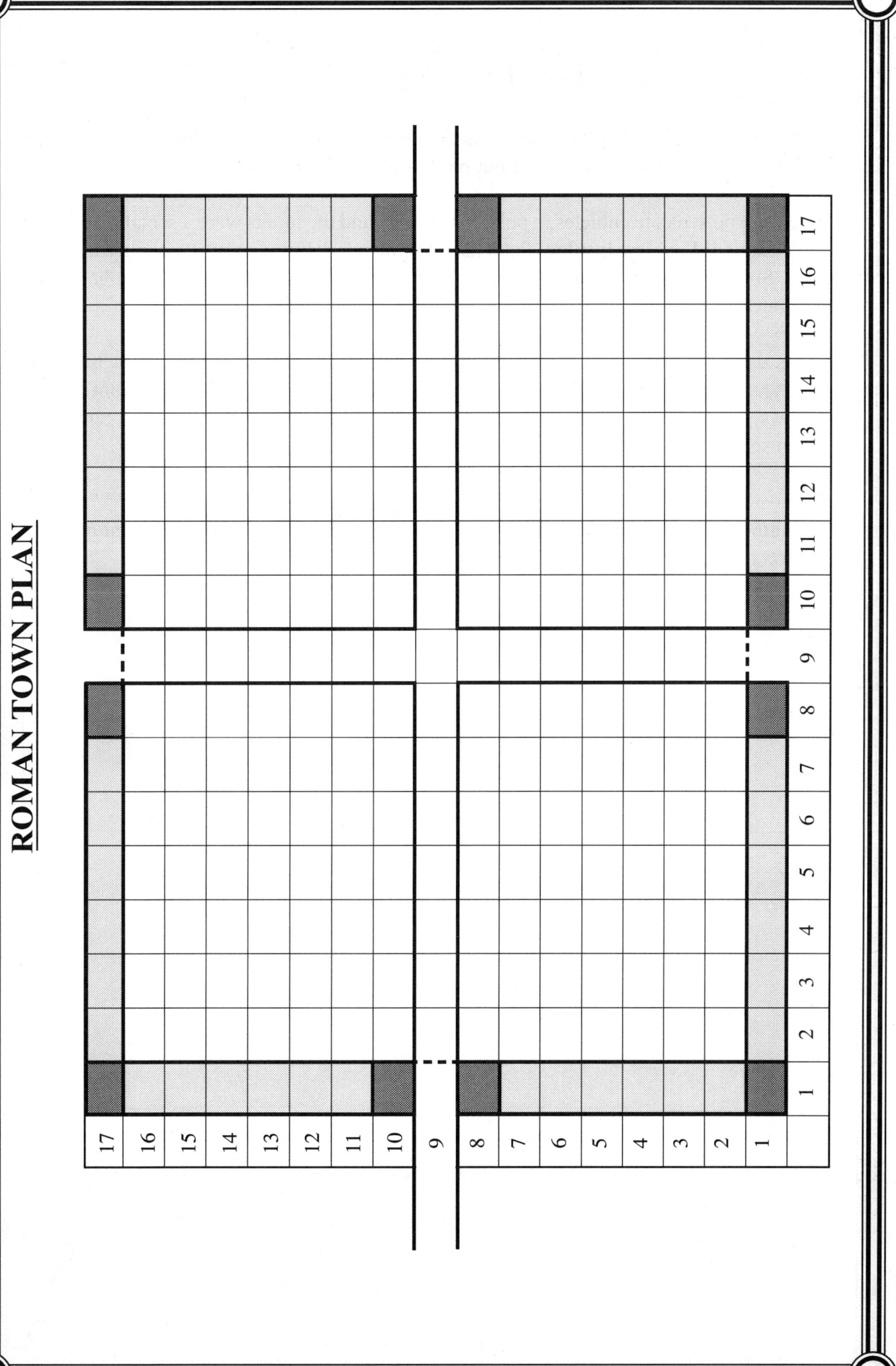

THE ROMAN TOILET

Roman toilets had stone seats. Water was flushed along a channel or drain, made of stone. The Romans did not use toilet paper but had sponges on sticks instead.

There were no separate cubicles in public lavatories and the toilets were a social place where people chatted! Very few **insulae** (flats) had their own toilets and so most people used public toilets. Some rich people had flushing toilets in their houses or villas, but they had to pay water rates.

Sewers were built of stone and were underground. They carried the town's waste away. Gutters ran along the streets, therefore rainwater and waste, which was poured from people's windows, ran into the sewers. Fragments of sponge have been found in the remains of Roman sewers in Britain.

1. Imagine you are a Roman visiting our time. What would you think of the public toilets today, compared to the Roman ones? Write your opinions below:

2. How can we prove that Romans used sponges on sticks instead of toilet paper?

THE CITY OF ROME

Try to match these famous buildings or monuments of Ancient Rome with the correct labels.

1. TRIUMPHAL ARCH
Arches were built to celebrate victories. There were several in Rome.

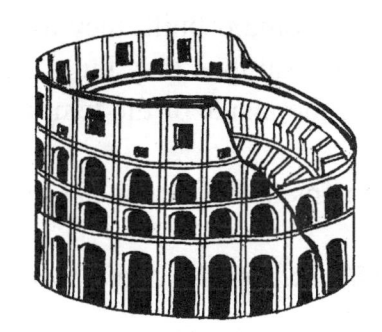

2. TRAJAN'S COLUMN
Trajan's campaigns in Dacia are sculpted on this column.

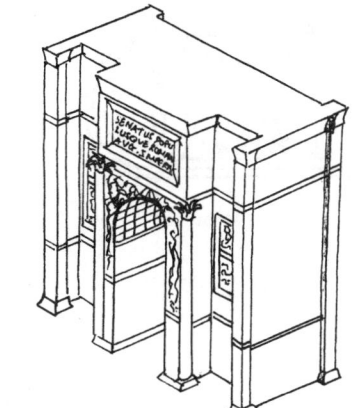

3. COLOSSEUM
Emperor Vespasian ordered the building of the Colosseum.

4. FORUM
The centre of trade and government in Rome.

5. TEMPLE OF AUGUSTUS
One of many temples in Rome. The Romans sometimes declared their Emperors to be gods too.

ROMAN ARCHITECTURE I

COLUMNS AND CAPITALS

When the Romans built, they used many ideas of the Greeks, but they adapted and altered them. For example, they built their temples in the same way as the Greeks, with columns, but made the inside of the temple, called the **cella**, larger.

The Romans used five kinds of capital for the tops of their columns.

Carefully cut out the capital and match it to its column on the next page.

Ionic

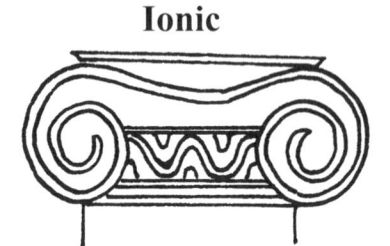

Doric

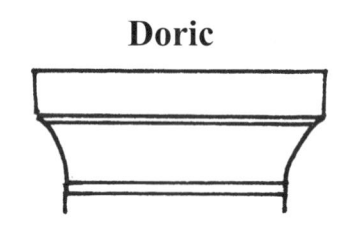

Corinthian

Composite

Tuscan

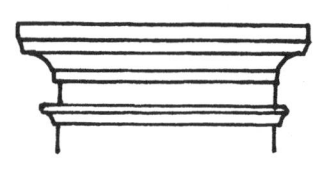

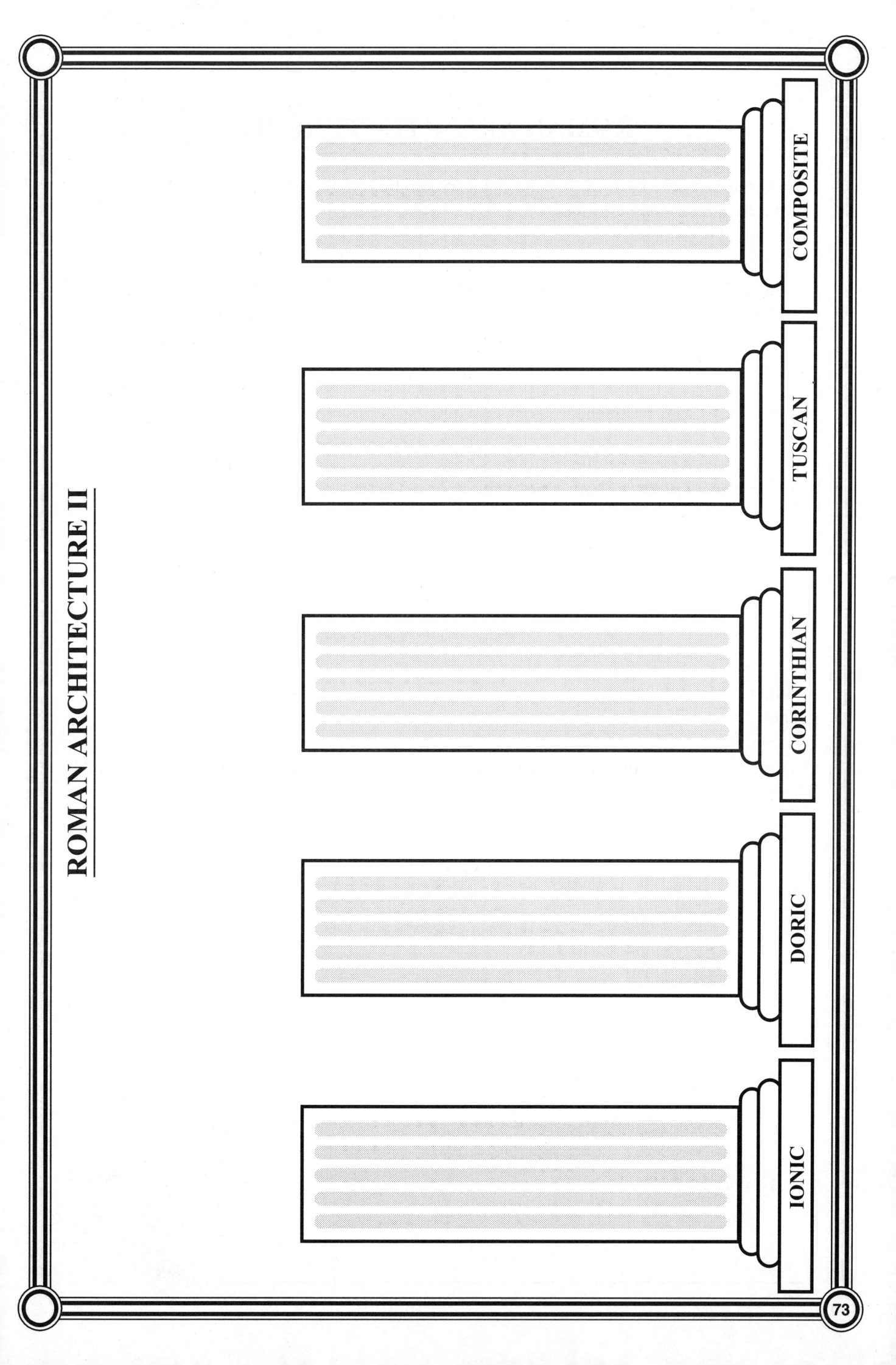

ROMAN ARCHITECTURE II

- IONIC
- DORIC
- CORINTHIAN
- TUSCAN
- COMPOSITE

ROMAN ARCHITECTURE III

The Romans used arches, vaults and domes when building. They carefully planned and built aqueducts and bridges.

An **Aqueduct** - supplied water to towns. It was made of a long line of arches joined together, slightly sloping, with a channel on the top to carry water. The water was carried through wood, lead, stone or pottery pipes to the public baths, lavatories and drinking fountains on street corners. Some private houses had a water supply for which they had to pay, and others used wells or streams.

A very large Roman aqueduct (Pont du Gard) still survives in Provence in the South of France.

Find or draw a picture of an aqueduct.

Bridges were built across rivers. They were usually made of wood or stone and some had arches.

A number of arches could form a vault and were sometimes used in bathhouses. From the idea of arches, the Romans developed the dome.

FIND OUT . . .
What was the Pantheon in Rome and what was important about its roof?
Write what you find below.

EVERYDAY LIFE IN ANCIENT ROMAN TIMES

ROMAN HOUSES I

Most Romans who lived in towns, lived in **insulae** or apartments. Some were small and cramped and others were more spacious. They were built mainly of wood and had about four or five floors. The richer people lived nearer to the ground, the poorer lived higher up in the building.

A Roman townhouse, called a **domus**, was usually L-shaped or had 3 or 4 wings built around a courtyard. Roman citizens and the wealthy lived in these kinds of houses. They kept servants and slaves, who would have had their own rooms. The houses of the rich had many features:

They were usually built of stone, brick or wood. Glass windows were a luxury and kept out the cold. They were not transparent but they let in some light. Some houses had shutters. The walls were plastered and painted and the floors had mosaics. The Romans heated their houses by having open fireplaces or a **hypocaust** (under-floor heating).

Some houses had bathrooms and those of the rich had piped water. Most houses did not have kitchens in towns and cities, although richer Romans did. Cooking was a fire risk as so many of the houses were made of wood. Most Romans ate take-away food, which they bought from street bars and stalls. Here they could buy hot bread, pies and meats. They would meet their friends here too.

The list below shows the rooms and features found in a Roman house.
Draw a plan of your own home on the sheet provided and label each room with its Latin name.

CULINA	Kitchen
CUBICULUM	Bedroom
PISCINA	Swimming Pool
LARARIUM	Shrine to the gods
ATRIUM	Entrance hallway
PERISTYLIUM	Courtyard with pillars
TRICLINIUM	Dining room
TABLINUM	Study
HORTUS	Garden

EVERYDAY LIFE IN ANCIENT ROMAN TIMES
ROMAN HOUSES II

PLAN OF MY HOME

List the rooms that you do not have in your house that the Romans had.

Are there any rooms that your house has that the Romans did not have?

EVERYDAY LIFE IN ANCIENT ROMAN TIMES

CENTRAL HEATING

In Rome, where the temperature was quite warm, central heating was used to heat water in bath houses. In the provinces, like Britain, where the climate was colder, the Romans put central heating or a **hypocaust** into their houses and country villas.

Brick pillars supported the floor. Fire-grates were built in the basement. When fires were lit in these grates, the warm air flowed between the pillars under the floors and up into ducts in the walls. The room became very hot. Romans had to wear special wooden shoes or sandals so that they did not burn their feet on the floors.

1. Using an orange or red coloured pencil, draw arrows to show how the heat flowed and how the room was warmed.

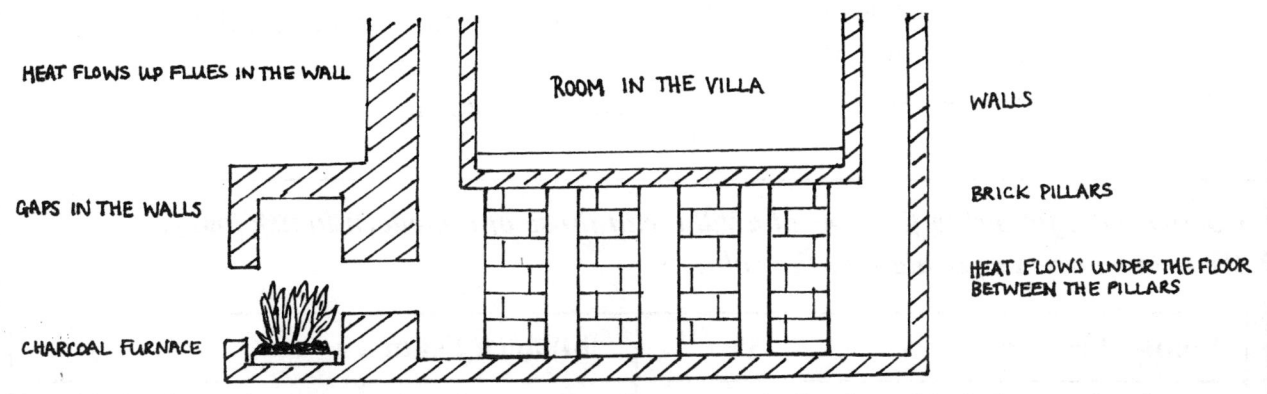

2. Think about the Roman heating system (hypocaust). In the table below, write down four disadvantages and advantages of this kind of heating:

Advantages	Disadvantages

3. How does it compare with the heating that you have in your home today?

EVERYDAY LIFE IN ANCIENT ROMAN TIMES

ROMAN VILLAS I

A villa was a country house in Roman times. Villas were usually owned by the rich who also lived in a **domus** or town house. They would visit their villas when they wanted a break from city-life. Villas were often farms and had a number of rooms and buildings.

In Italy, villas on an estate produced olive oil and made wine.

In the provinces, like Britain, villas tended to be farming centres but also some were important for other industries, such as pottery, metalwork or quarrying.

A few villas were luxurious palaces that were used just for their owner's pleasure and relaxation.

Every villa was different. They tended to be built around a central courtyard. There was often a **triclinium** or dining room, bedrooms, a kitchen, outbuildings - such as barns, storerooms and offices. Villas were made up of separate rooms and corridors, giving privacy. The more luxurious villas were beautifully decorated with mosaics, painted walls, glazed windows, and were well furnished. Some had a **hypocaust** (central heating).

Compare the following features of a villa with those of a modern house today.
Write the correct equivalent in the column.

Roman Feature	Modern Feature
Fountain, well or spring	
Bath house	
	Carpet
Wall plaster with painted frescoes	
	Brick walls
	Outside shed and garage
Window shutters	
	Central heating boiler / radiators
	Microwave oven

Find Out . . .
about Hadrian's Villa in Tivoli, near to Rome.

EVERYDAY LIFE IN ANCIENT ROMAN TIMES

ROMAN VILLAS II

Imagine that you are a Celt in Britain, who lives in a simple round house. You have just visited a Roman Villa for the first time.
Write down what you would tell your family about it and what your views would be.

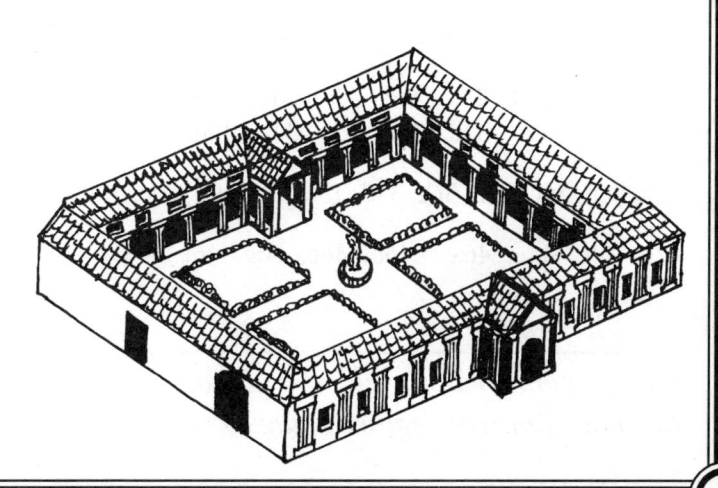

EVERYDAY LIFE IN ANCIENT ROMAN TIMES

ROMAN MOSAICS

We have carpets, tiles, lino or wood on the floors of our houses. The Romans laid mosaics on their floors. They were highly decorated patterns or pictures, made of tiny pieces of coloured stones or marble, called **tesserae**. Mosaic-makers were highly skilled artists.

Follow the co-ordinates on this page, and carefully colour in the squares on the next page, to reveal the picture and message in the mosaic. Take care! What do you think it means?

PICTURE (DARK GREY)

19z → 22z, 18y → 23y, 16x → 23x, 18w → 23w, 15v → 23v, 19u → 22u, 20t → 21t, 23t → 37t, 22s → 35s,
21r → 34r, 20q → 34q, 20p → 34p, 20o → 34o,
20n → 34n, 21m → 33m,
21l → 23l, 31l → 33l
21k, 22k, 32k, 33k,
21j, 22j, 32j, 33j,
21i, 22i, 32i, 33i,
21h, 22h, 32h, 33h
20g → 22g, 31g → 33g,
36u, 37u, 38u,
38v, 39v, 40v,
40w, 41w, 42w,
42x, 43x,
43y, 44y, 44z.

LIGHT BROWN
16l, 15l, 15m, 14k, 13j, 12i, 11g, 11h, 10h.

BLACK   **RED**
20x, 15x.   23u, 22t, 21s.

HELPFUL TIPS

The → means colour all the boxes between the two numbers.

For example: 19z → 22z means colour squares 19z, 20z, 21z and 22z.

Cross off the co-ordinates when you have done them.

MESSAGE- RED/ORANGE.
5b, 5c, 5d, 6a, 6e, 7a, 7e, 8b, 8d.   10a, 10b, 10c, 10d, 11e, 12e, 11c, 12c, 13a, 13b, 13c, 13d.

15b, 15c, 15d, 15e, 16a, 17a, 18b, 18c, 18d, 18e.   20a → 23a, 20b, 20c, 20d, 20e, 21c, 22c, 21e, 22e, 23e.

26b, 26c, 26d, 27a, 27e, 28a, 28e, 29b, 29d,
31a, 31b, 31c, 31d, 32e, 33e, 34a, 34b, 34c, 34d, 32c, 33c.

36a, 36b, 36c, 36d, 36e, 37d, 38c, 39a, 39b, 39c, 39d, 39e. 41a, 41b, 41c, 41d, 41e, 42a, 42c, 42e, 43a, 43c.

43e, 44a, 44e, 46a.   46b, 46c, 46d, 46e, 47d, 48c, 49d, 50a, 50b, 50c, 50d, 50e.

Design your own mosaic, like the ones above, using co-ordinates and give it to a friend to solve. You will require squared paper.

EVERYDAY LIFE IN ANCIENT ROMAN TIMES - MOSAICS

Using the co-ordinates on the previous page, colour in the correct tesserae to reveal a picture and message. What does it mean?

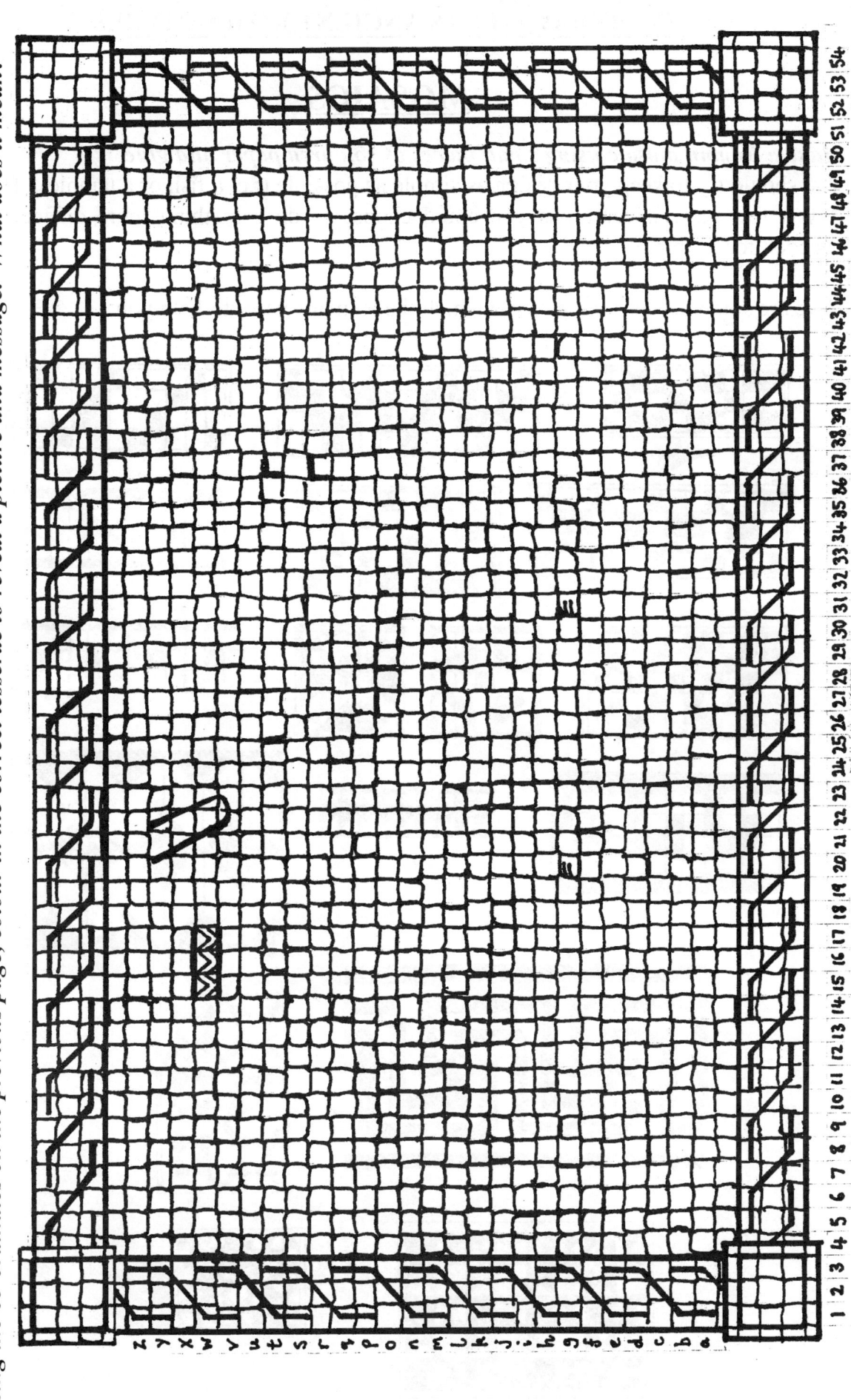

EVERYDAY LIFE IN ANCIENT ROMAN TIMES

MOSAICS

Make a Roman mosaic using small pieces of coloured paper and glue.
You should try to keep your design as simple as possible (i.e. a fish or a temple). However if you feel more adventurous you could choose to do something more difficult, like a peacock for example!

Here are some designs and patterns which the Romans used, to help you.

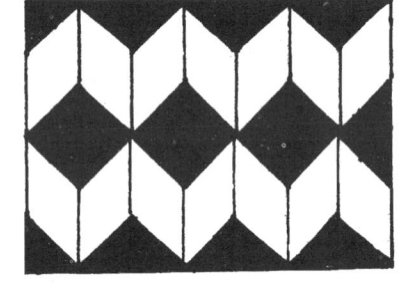

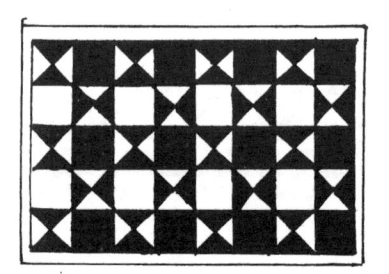

EVERYDAY LIFE IN ANCIENT ROMAN TIMES

ROMAN GARDENS

Romans loved gardens and many houses had two outside areas. They had a pillared courtyard called an **atrium**, which was where guests were welcomed and business could be carried out. Houses could also have a courtyard, containing a garden, which would be for relaxing in. Here there were plants, statues, fountains and fish ponds. In Britain, there may have been apple and pear trees, grape vines, rose bushes and herbs.

In villas, farmers grew carrots, peas, beans, wheat, onions and leeks. They produced bread, milk, cheese and meat for the local town.

Archaeology shows us that the Romans liked to arrange flower beds and paths in their gardens in a formal design. They used a lattice fencing and box bushes clipped into different shapes. The Romans liked roses, lilies, violets, anemones and poppies. They also grew myrtle and oleander. The Romans' favourite trees were cypresses and plane trees. One Roman loved his plane trees so much that he watered them with wine!

Cut out the boxes below and re-arrange them to form a picture of a Roman garden. Colour it in.

How does this garden compare with our gardens today?

EVERYDAY LIFE IN ANCIENT ROMAN TIMES
ROMAN CITIZENS I

Using your dictionary, find out what a citizen is. Write a definition here:

In Roman times, *only men* could be Roman citizens. There were three classes of citizen: The **patricians** who were the richest, **equites** who were businessmen and **plebeians** who were the poorest. Citizens had several rights:

ROMAN CITIZENS COULD:
- become citizens at the age of 14 years
- vote
- serve in the army
- hold official positions in government
- own their own property
- become legally married
- appeal if they were charged with a crime

Commands shall be obeyed and fair. If a citizen is found guilty or disobedient, a magistrate can punish him with imprisonment, fines or lashes. This is unless an equal or more powerful person forbids it, when a citizen appeals to him.

CICERO (106 - 43B.C.)

1. What could a citizen do if he disagreed with his punishment? Do you think that this was right?

2. In the space below, write down who can be a British citizen today and what rights they have:

EVERYDAY LIFE IN ANCIENT ROMAN TIMES

ROMAN CITIZENS II

3. What is similar and what is different about the rights of citizens in Roman and modern times? Write your ideas below:

SIMILARITIES	DIFFERENCES

A Roman Official wrote the excerpt below. It tells us about the punishment that the Romans gave to people of different social ranks.

NON-CITIZENS

Those who start a riot are, according to their rank, either crucified, thrown to the wild beasts or sent to an island . . . Those who dig up boundary stones, if they are slaves, are sent to work in the mines. If they are humble, they have to labour on public buildings. If they are of superior rank, one third of their property is taken away and they are sent to live in exile.

Written by a Roman Official

4. Discuss whether you think it was fair of the Romans to treat people so differently? Does this happen in our society today?

EVERYDAY LIFE IN ANCIENT ROMAN TIMES

THE ROMAN FAMILY

A Roman family was quite large. Rich families also had a large number of slaves. We know from writing on tombstones that some families were close and that they showed grief when members of the family died.

THE FATHER (paterfamilias)
The father was head of the household. Everyone had to obey his orders and he had authority over his family and his slaves. He was a citizen.

THE MOTHER
Sometimes girls were married at the age of 13 years. A wife always had to obey her husband, and if he died, she was then under the control of her son or another male relative. A mother's main job was to look after the house. She had to cook, spin and weave cloth too. Once she had children, if she survived the birth, she had to look after them as well. Wealthy women had slaves who did most of these household jobs. Women were not allowed to be citizens and therefore could not vote, but were allowed to go to entertainments. Women lived for an average of 30 years.

Women in Ancient Britain had much more freedom than the Roman women. They could fight in battle and took over their husband's responsibilities when he died.

CHILDREN
The father decided whether a new child would be introduced into the family or not. Sons were very important in Roman families because they would be needed for business and public life. Daughters were sometimes left to die. When children were accepted into the family, offerings were made to the gods. Once a boy was nine days old, he would be named and given a special charm called a **bulla** to wear around his neck. When he started to walk, he was dressed in a striped toga. As soon as he needed to shave, the first hairs from his beard were place into a box and were dedicated to the gods, to thank them for turning him into a man. A boy was grown up at the age of about 14 years, when he became a citizen.

SLAVES
Many rich families could buy slaves and own them. They would cook and clean and carry out hard work on the land. Sometimes they were treated very badly, but some were lucky and had kind masters who treated them well. Sometimes a master would free a slave if he had served him well, or a slave could save up the money he had been given by his master, and could use this to buy his own freedom.

1. *Discuss the differences between our families today and the Roman family. Write down all the main differences and illustrate them.*

2. *Would you have liked to be a member of a Roman family? Which member would you have preferred to be? Explain your answers.*

EVERYDAY LIFE IN ANCIENT ROMAN TIMES

CHILDREN AND EDUCATION

Wealthy Roman children were educated at school or by private tutors at home, but poorer children were needed by their families to work.

Richer children began school at about six or seven years old and they attended a **ludus** or primary school. They left this school at about the age of eleven. There were about twelve children in a class. They learned the alphabet and how to read and write and they practised their writing on wooden wax tablets, using a **stylus,** or on bits of pottery. Older children had to learn the works of famous authors and recite them. They were also allowed to write on papyrus scrolls with a pen. Teachers were often Greek slaves who were educated.

At twelve years old, girls began to prepare for marriage but boys went to a **grammaticus** or a secondary school teacher who taught them music, astronomy, philosophy, geometry, geography, history and Greek and Roman literature.

A teacher was strict and would commonly punish the boys by caning them, for disobedience, bad manners or for not learning their work quickly enough.

From sixteen years old, the boys were taught how to do public speaking by a **rhetor,** so that they could become politicians or lawyers.

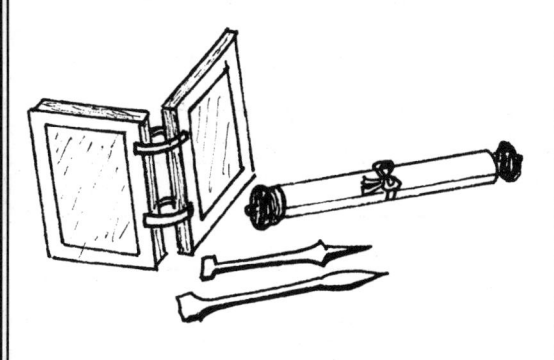

> People passing . . . could hear the boys chanting their lesson . . . Every now and then someone would get a good beating . . . School was held between October and the end of June . . . The teacher's pay was so low it was hardly worth mentioning. However, parents refused to pay the fees if their sons did not learn anything. To make sure they received their money some teachers pushed their students very hard. The cane was always ready, keeping class in order.
> ANON

Activities:

1. Write down the main differences and similarities that you can think of between your own school and the Roman schools above. Discuss these with a partner.

2. Imagine that you are a Roman school child.
   Write about your experiences of your school.
You may wish to include the following:
- Different stages of education
- The behaviour of the pupils
- Any other information (i.e. how hard it was to learn and recite poetry etc.)
- The subjects taught at the different levels
- The teachers

3. Write your own end of year school report as if you were at a Roman school.

EVERYDAY LIFE IN ANCIENT ROMAN TIMES
ROMAN NUMERALS

The Romans wrote their numbers using symbols, called numerals. They are still used in some places, even today. Here are some of the important numbers.

I	=	1
II	=	2
III	=	3
IV	=	4
V	=	5
VI	=	6
VII	=	7
VIII	=	8
IX	=	9
X	=	10
XI	=	11
XII	=	12
XIII	=	13
XIV	=	14
XV	=	15
XVI	=	16
XVII	=	17
XVIII	=	18
XIX	=	19
XX	=	20
XXV	=	25
XXX	=	30
XL	=	40
L	=	50
LX	=	60
LXX	=	70
LXXX	=	80
XC	=	90
C	=	100
D	=	500
M	=	1000

Find out and write down where you have seen Roman numerals still used in today's society.

Work out the following numerals and write them in numbers:

1. XXII _____
2. XLIX _____
3. LXXIV _____
4. LXIII _____
5. LXXXVI _____
6. CXVII _____
7. CCXCIX _____
8. DXLVII _____
9. DCCLXXVII _____
10. MCM _____

Calculate these sums and write the answers in numerals:

1. VII + IV = _____
2. XII + IX = _____
3. XVI − VII = _____
4. L + XLIX = _____
5. D − C = _____
6. M ÷ L = _____

Now make up some Roman numeral sums of your own in the space below, and give them to a friend to solve. Make sure you know the answers to your questions!

EVERYDAY LIFE IN ANCIENT ROMAN TIMES

THE LATIN LANGUAGE

The Romans spoke Latin. Since the time of the Romans, Latin has been used by doctors, lawyers, clergymen and scientists, for reading and writing. Many English words come from Latin. Look at the words in the list below. They are Latin words which are used in English.

alter	-	other
ante	-	before
aqua	-	water
circum	-	around
cum	-	with
contra	-	against
extra	-	outside
inter	-	between
magnus	-	large
malus	-	bad, wrong
manus	-	hand
post	-	after
sub	-	under
super	-	above

Underline the Latin part in the English words. Write down what these words mean:

alternative _____

submarine _____

international _____

malfunction _____

communication _____

circumference _____

Using the Latin words in the list above, find other words in English that come from the Latin. They may also start with these words as prefixes.

Word	Meaning of the Word

Find Out . . .

These abbreviations are Latin and are used today. *Find out what they mean and where you would find them today.*

P.S.   (post scriptum)
A.D.   (anno domini)
a.m.   (ante meridiem)
p.m.   (post meridiem)

Did you know . . . that the Romans invented the calendar?

Januarius	Maius	September
Februarius	Junius	October
Martius	Julius	November
Aprilis	Augustus	December

Find out what these words mean.

EVERYDAY LIFE IN ANCIENT ROMAN TIMES
MONEY AND TRADE

The Romans used coins, usually made of bronze or copper, but some were made of silver and gold. Every coin had a picture of the Emperor's head on it.

AUREUS	- a gold coin.
DENARIUS	- a silver coin. One aureus was worth 25 denarii.
SESTERTIUS	- a bronze coin. There were four sestertii in one denarius.
DUPONDIUS	- a brass or bronze coin. This was worth half a sestertius.
AS	- a copper coin. Four of these made a sestertius.
SEMIS	- there were 2 of these to an as.
QUADRANS	- made of copper. There were four quadrans to an as.

Banks became important in the Roman Empire as trading spread. Huge numbers of goods were traded between Rome and other countries in the Empire. Roman roads were used to import and export goods quickly.

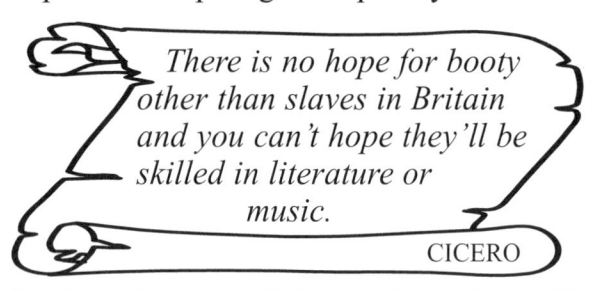

There is no hope for booty other than slaves in Britain and you can't hope they'll be skilled in literature or music.
— CICERO

Britain was a source for grain, cattle, gold, silver and iron. They are exported with animal skins, slaves and hunting dogs.
— STRATO

Look at the map of the products from all over the Empire.

Make a list of the produce that was available from these countries.

SPAIN:

BRITAIN:

GREECE:

GAUL:

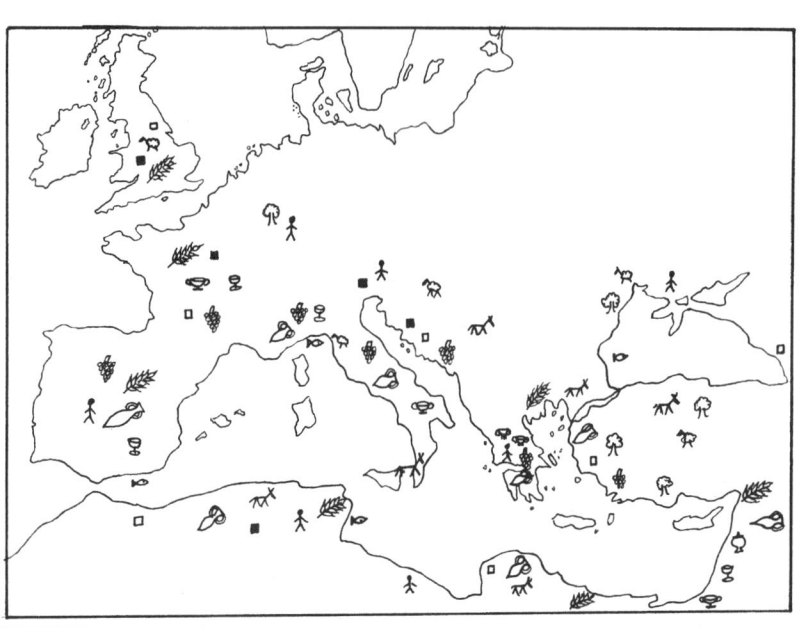

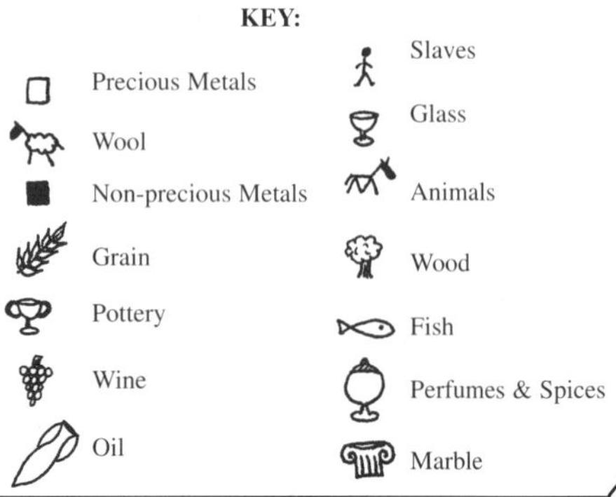

KEY:
- Precious Metals
- Wool
- Non-precious Metals
- Grain
- Pottery
- Wine
- Oil
- Slaves
- Glass
- Animals
- Wood
- Fish
- Perfumes & Spices
- Marble

EVERYDAY LIFE IN ANCIENT ROMAN TIMES

ROMAN CLOTHING I

Cut out the clothes on the next page and dress the Roman family below. Label the clothes with the correct Roman names.

EVERYDAY LIFE IN ANCIENT ROMAN TIMES

ROMAN CLOTHING II

Women: wore a wool or linen tunic. Over this they wore a brightly coloured **stola**, which was a long robe. They wrapped a **palla** around them.

Men: wore a tunic in different colours. Important men wore **togas**. If they were senators, they had a purple stripe on their toga.

Boys: wore a tunic and sometimes a **toga praetexta**. They also wore a bulla.
Girls: wore a tunic and sometimes a **stola**.

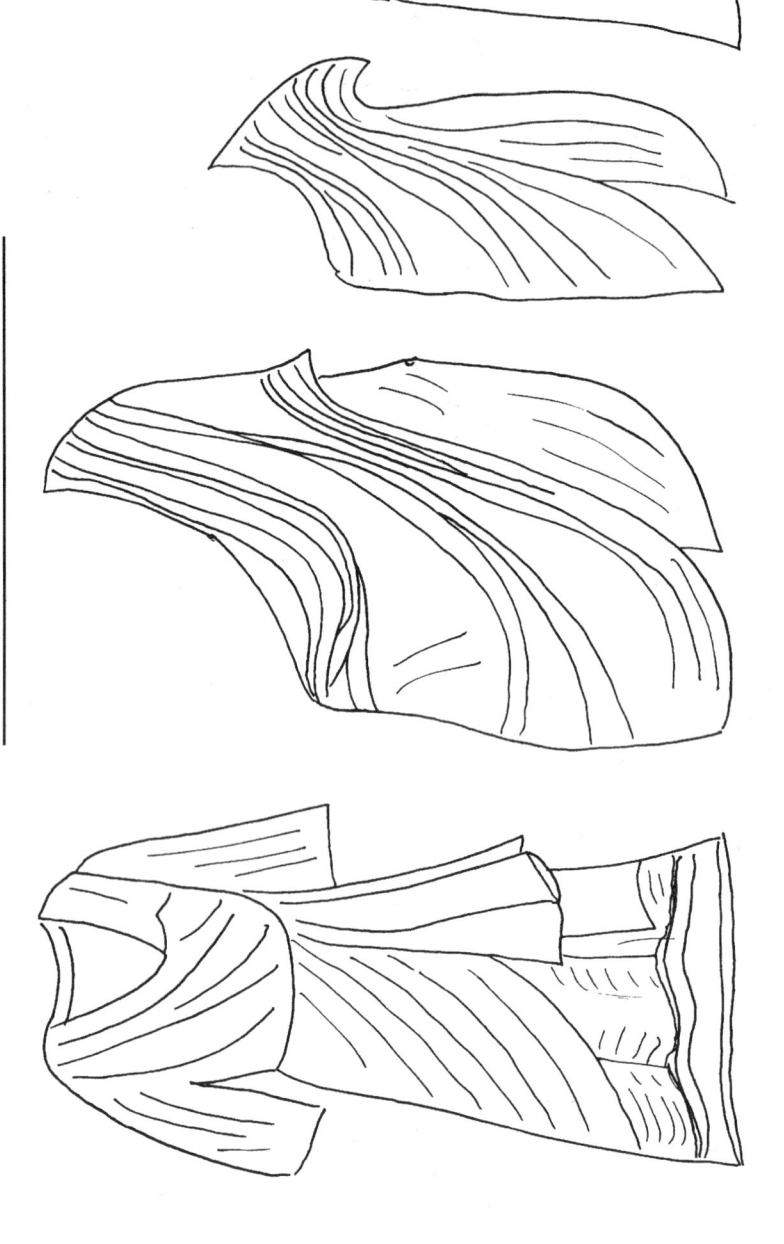

Everyone wore leather sandals on their feet.

EVERYDAY LIFE IN ANCIENT ROMAN TIMES

ROMAN FASHION

Hairstyles
Both men and women curled their hair with hot tongs. They also put oil and grease on to it to make it grow. Women were helped by slaves to dye their hair. They sometimes wore wigs and tied their hair into a bun or put it in plaits. They also sprayed their hair with perfume. Men tended to have their beards shaved at a barber's shop, which was a place to meet friends and to chat. The barber did not use oil or soap and cuts were common.

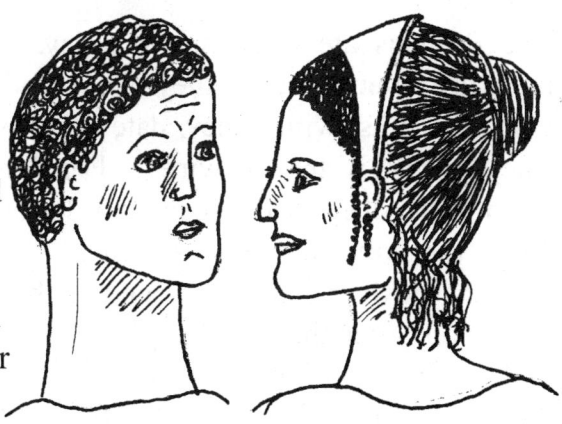

Makeup
Women liked to wear makeup. They stored their makeup in tiny bottles and pots. It was fashionable to have a white face, so women used powdered chalk or white lead. They darkened their eyelids with ash or squashed flies and for their lips and cheeks they used the sediment from red wine or a plant dye, called **fundus**. Rich women wore perfume made from myrrh and spices or rose petals.

1. Follow the instructions and put the correct makeup on this Roman Woman:

Jewellery
The Romans wore jewellery. They used metals, such as gold, silver, bronze and iron and decorated this with precious and semi-precious stones, like emeralds, pearls and sapphires. They also used polished glass. Both Roman men and women wore rings and also brooches, to fasten their cloaks. Brooches were often shaped like animals, to bring luck. Some animals were symbols of certain gods; for example, the owl was Minerva's animal.

Women also wore necklaces, earrings, anklets, brooches and hairpins. These could be highly decorated and many have been found all over the Roman Empire.

2. Using silver or gold foil, card, glue and some coloured sequins (for precious stones), make your own Roman jewellery.

EVERYDAY LIFE IN ANCIENT ROMAN TIMES

FOOD AND DRINK I

The Romans ate three meals a day. For breakfast, **jentaculum**, they ate bread or wheat biscuits, with honey, dates or olives. They drank water or wine. For lunch, **prandium**, they had bread and leftovers from the previous evening meal. The Romans ate their main meal, **cena**, in the late afternoon, after their visit to the baths. For poorer Romans, meals consisted of wheat, made into a porridge. They also had cheese, made from goat's milk, eggs, onions and olives. Meat was sometimes provided after animal sacrifices. Meals could not be cooked in their own homes because of the risk of fire, so Romans bought their food from food stalls, or shops, or from a tavern.

Dinner Parties

The very rich had lavish dinner parties and invited friends and important people for the **cena**. The rich had large kitchens which were well equipped. Romans did not use knives and forks, but ate using their fingers or spoons. The Romans did not sit on chairs, but reclined on couches and ate from low tables, which were arranged on three sides of the central table. Musicians, acrobats and dancers performed during the feast.

The Cena

This meal usually had three courses, but some could have up to seven courses!

Did you know ?
that a recipe book written by a Roman called Apicus survives? It tells us about the foods that the Romans ate and how they were cooked.
Apicus tells us that Romans spread spicy fish sauce on their meat and fish! They also ate dormice and lark's tongues.

Typical Food served at a Cena

First Course *(gustatio)*
Salad, radishes, oysters or shellfish, sardines, snails and eggs or mushrooms.
Wine: **mulsum**, which was sweetened with honey.

Second Course
This could include up to seven dishes, including meat (boar, venison, kid, sow's udders, sheep, pork, hare, beef, goat, dormice etc.) fish and poultry, such as goose and peacock etc. These were served with vegetables and sauces.

Third Course *(secundae mensae) - dessert*
Fruit, nuts, dates, figs and honey cakes were served.
Wines were served throughout these courses.

EVERYDAY LIFE IN ANCIENT ROMAN TIMES

FOOD AND DRINK II

A Roman slave has just bought the following foods for a dinner party. Help him to sort them out and make a 3-course menu for the dinner. *Use the space below to write your menu and to help you plan your meal. Use the information on page 94.*

dates   chicken   vegetables   honey

nuts   wine   fish sauce

figs   mushrooms   peacock

tuna   snails

CENA

Below is some of the equipment that was used for a dinner party or cena:

Amphorae	-	wine or oil storage jars which had pointed bottoms
Storage Jars	-	were used to keep olive oil
Honey Pots	-	honey was used to sweeten food, as there was no sugar
Cooking Pots	-	these were earthenware or bronze pots
Serving Plates	-	were made of glass, pottery, silver or gold
Silver Drinking Cups		
Samian Red Pottery Bowls		
Knives		
Pestle and Mortar	-	A pestle was used to grind food to a powder in a bowl called a mortar. It was used to make sauces.

EVERYDAY LIFE IN ANCIENT ROMAN TIMES

ENTERTAINMENT - THE THEATRE

The Romans enjoyed different kinds of entertainment. They regularly visited the theatre, races, games and gladiator fights, usually on festival days.

The Theatre

The Romans enjoyed going to the theatre. Actors wore masks to make them easy to identify and to show whether they were meant to be young or old, gods, good or evil characters. They also wore platform shoes to make them look taller. Theatres were large, built in a semi-circle, and could seat thousands of people in the audience. The poorer the people were, the higher they sat in the theatre. The best seats, in front of the stage, were reserved for senators. This area was called the orchestra. People bought cushions to sit on to make the seats comfortable. The audience was noisy and clapped, booed and hissed. It was mainly men who became actors, but women did start performing later. The Romans had complicated machinery for changing the scenery on the stage.

Label the following areas on the Roman theatre plan below:
stage, seating, orchestra

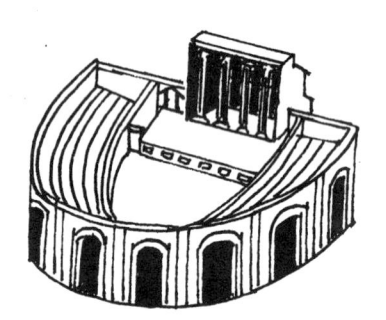

How to make your own Roman dramatic mask.

(This activity should be done in pairs).

What you will need:

a round balloon	paint
newspaper	varnish
cold water paste	wool
scissors or a craft knife	elastic

(i) First of all, blow up and fasten a round balloon.
(ii) Mix the cold water paste to a thick consistency.
(iii) Shred the newspaper into smallish strips.
(iv) Dip the shredded newspaper into the paste and cover the entire balloon evenly with several layers of paper. Make sure that the newspaper is very smooth and does not buckle.
(v) Leave the covered balloon to dry.
(vi) Pop the balloon carefully, and cut the solid papier mâché shape in half, lengthways, to make two mask bases.
(vii) With more pasted newspaper, build up a nose, cheeks, eyebrows, chin and lips. Be careful not to get the mask too wet again at this stage, as it could collapse.
(viii) When all is dry, carefully cut out a hole for the mouth and smaller holes for the eyes using scissors or a craft knife.
(ix) Paint the mask with bright colours. Add wool to it for hair, or if preferred this could also be painted. When dry finish off with a coat of varnish.
(x) Elastic can be fastened to each side of the mask, which can then be worn!

EVERYDAY LIFE IN ANCIENT ROMAN TIMES

ENTERTAINMENT - THE RACES & GLADIATOR FIGHTS I

RACES

Chariot races were very popular and took place in a racecourse called the circus. Each race lasted about seven laps. Each lap was about 600 metres long. The rounded ends of the course were the most dangerous, as chariots could overturn. The largest racecourse in Rome was called the **Circus Maximus.**

There were usually four teams of chariot racers. The crowds supported their team and even wore the team's colours (white, blue, red or green), like our football teams. Competitors could however be killed. Winners won a lot of money; one was Diocles, who won several races and became a millionaire. Slaves who were racers could be freed if they raced well.

GLADIATOR FIGHTS

The Romans enjoyed watching the gladiator fights, and shows were usually free of charge. Gladiators were trained slaves, prisoners or criminals who fought each other as well as wild animals. All fights usually continued until someone died, although the wounded soldier could appeal for mercy. The official at the fight, or the emperor himself if he was present, would listen to the views of the crowd and then decide if the man should survive or die. The 'thumbs up' signal meant that the man should survive.

Later, unarmed Christians were led into the arena to be attacked by hungry lions and other fierce animals, for the crowd's entertainment.

There were five different kinds of gladiators: **retiarius, murmillo, samnite** (in Latin - samnis)**, secutor** and **thracian** (in Latin - thrax)**.** They could be told apart by their costumes and their weapons. A successful gladiator could become rich and was awarded a crown and great praise. If he was given a wooden sword, this meant he could become free. He could then become a trainer at a gladiator school.

EVERYDAY LIFE IN ANCIENT ROMAN TIMES
ENTERTAINMENT - GLADIATOR FIGHTS II

Read the views of Romans who wrote about the gladiator fights and answer the questions:

1. What does Martial tell us about the job of a gladiator?

> He plunged his spear . . . into a bear, king of the beasts, rushing fast towards him . . . and he killed a lion . . . and with a deep wound, he killed a rushing leopard. He won the prize of honour, yet his strength remained unbroken.
>
> MARTIAL Epigrams (80 A.D.)

2. What did Seneca think of the games?

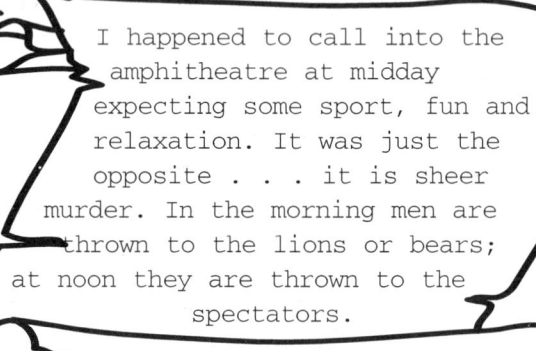

> I happened to call into the amphitheatre at midday expecting some sport, fun and relaxation. It was just the opposite . . . it is sheer murder. In the morning men are thrown to the lions or bears; at noon they are thrown to the spectators.
>
> SENECA (1st Century A.D.)

> Alypius himself watched; he shouted, and took away with him a mad desire which made him not want only to return but even . . . to drag others along.
>
> ST. AUGUSTINE (4th Century A.D.)

3. What did Alypius think of the games? Do you think that St Augustine approves of him?

4. What does this evidence tell us about the views of Romans?

EVERYDAY LIFE IN ANCIENT ROMAN TIMES
ENTERTAINMENT - GLADIATOR FIGHTS III

Activities:

1. ***Find out as much as you can about the Colosseum in Rome. Make a small factbook or guidebook of the Colosseum.***

   You may like to make the booklet using the instructions below:

Fold a piece of A4 paper in half, lengthways.
Now fold it in half and then in half again.
Open the page up to A4 again and this time fold it across the middle to make it A5.
From the folded side, cut down the middle to the halfway point.
Open up again and re-fold lengthways.
Push the two ends together so that the centre opens up and fold it into a book.

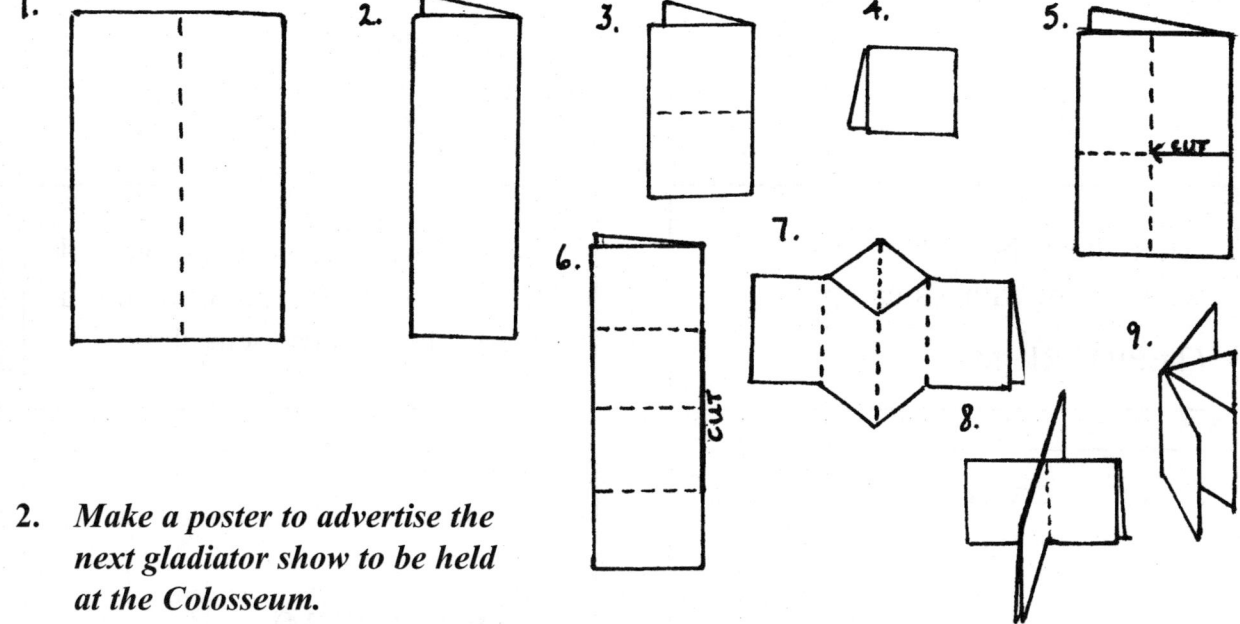

2. ***Make a poster to advertise the next gladiator show to be held at the Colosseum.***

In pairs, discuss all the information that you would need to put on to your poster to inform your fellow Romans about the show and to encourage them to attend.

Write your ideas in the box below:

EVERYDAY LIFE IN ANCIENT ROMAN TIMES
THE ROMAN BATHS

Roman Baths were like our modern leisure centres. Many Romans spent much of their time relaxing at the baths. Not only was it a place to get clean but it was also a chance to meet friends. The emperors built baths to show off how much wealth and power they had. The baths were often decorated ornately with marble and even gold. When the Romans invaded Britain, they built baths in their towns, like the ones in Rome.

Cut out and arrange the following in the correct order that they visit each of the rooms. Illustrate each section like a cartoon strip.

You may wish to use the plan on the next page to help you with the order.

FLAVIUS and MARCUS are visiting the baths today.

After their sport, they rest in the warm room with a small pool.

(TEPIDARIUM)

Slaves scrape off their sweat and dirt in the next room, using a strigil. This makes them clean.

Feeling very sweaty but clean after the hot room, Flavius and his son cool down by jumping into the cold bath. (FRIGIDARIUM)

They take off their clothes in the changing room.

(APODYTERIUM)

Finally they enjoy a relaxing swim in the main pool.

(PISCINA)

Following their rest, Flavius and his son go into the hot room. (CALDARIUM). The steam makes them sweat again.

After changing, they play ball and wrestle in the exercise yard.

(BASILICA)

Flavius and his son Marcus have decided to visit the baths today.

EVERYDAY LIFE IN ANCIENT ROMAN TIMES

LEISURE - THE BATHS

LOOK AT THE PLAN OF THE BATHS. Fill in the Latin name for each area.

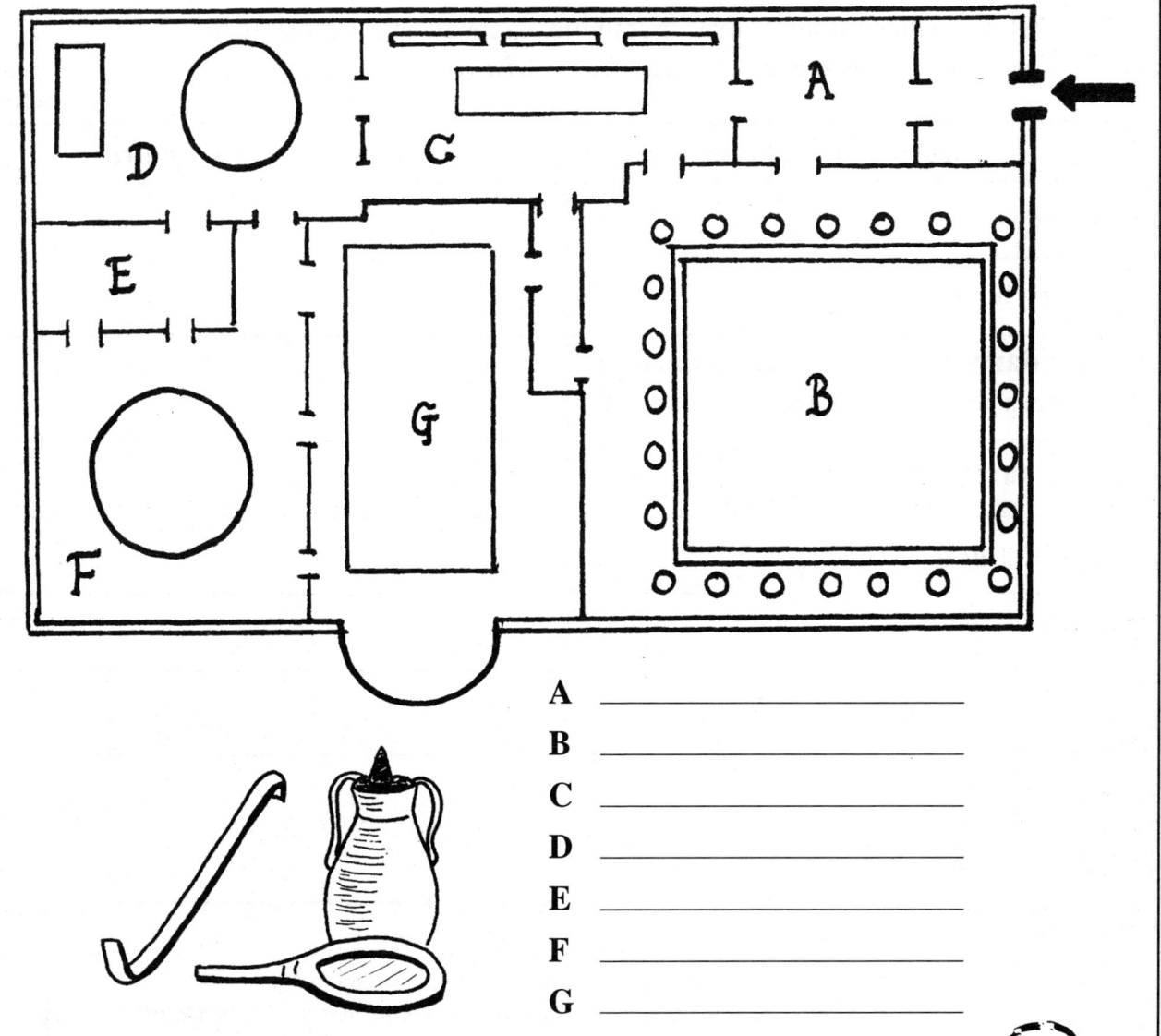

A _____
B _____
C _____
D _____
E _____
F _____
G _____

RESEARCH AREAS

1. *Find out what a STRIGIL looks like & how it worked. What did the Romans use for soap?*

2. *Find out what the Romans wore when they bathed.*

3. *Where are the most famous Roman baths in Britain? What can you find out about them?*

4. *Roman baths were places where some people hoped that the water would cure their illnesses. Try to find out where (in Europe) people who are ill today go to bathe and drink the medicinal waters.*

EVERYDAY LIFE IN ANCIENT ROMAN TIMES
THE ROMAN BATHS

The Roman baths were a little like a modern leisure centre.

Listed below are the different areas or activities in an ancient Roman bath.
Write down what the modern comparison in a leisure centre would be.

Ancient Roman Baths	Modern Leisure Centre
basilica	
apodyterium	
frigidarium, tepidarium, caldarium (places where the Romans washed)	
piscina	
market hall	
food stalls	
latrines	

Seneca wrote about living above the baths in Rome in about A.D.63.
Read what he said about it.

> I live just above the public baths.
> You can imagine what it is like. Ah! It is nauseating!
> To start with, there are musclemen, doing exercises and heaving lead weights around with grunts and groans. Then there are the layabouts having cheap massages.
> I can hear the slaps on someone's shoulders now.
> Next there is the noise of a yob or a thief being arrested and the show-off who likes the sound of his own voice in the bath. And what about the ones who jump in the pool, making an enormous splash as they hit the water?

Did Seneca like living above the baths? How can you tell?

EVERYDAY LIFE IN ANCIENT ROMAN TIMES

ROMAN RELIGION I

The Romans did not believe in just one god, but in a large number of gods. Religion was very important to the Romans and they were very superstitious people. For example, they believed that a flock of birds, a storm or a strange-shaped cloud told people about the mood of the gods. Fortune-tellers or soothsayers, called **haruspices**, looked at the guts of a dead animal to discover good or bad news. The Romans thought that the best way to please the gods was to make animal sacrifices.

Romans built temples to worship their gods. Each god or goddess had his or her own temple.

A DEFIXIO

The Romans also asked the gods to help them, if they wanted to accuse or punish someone else of doing something to them. They wrote a curse, a **defixio** or **exsecratio** about that person on a piece of pot or lead and left it in the temple, like the one below. The message was written backwards to add to the magic and secrecy of the curse.

Try to work out what this curse to Neptune says, by reading each word backwards:

> DEUS NEPTUNE
> MY STOLEN HAS WHO HIM CURSE I
> WOMAN OR MAN WHETHER CLOAK
> FREE OR SLAVE. NEPTUNE MY INFLICT
> MAN THIS UPON ILLNESS. NOT HE MAY
> RETURN HAS HE UNTIL NIGHT AT SLEEP
> TEMPLE YOUR TO CLOAK MY.

Write your own curse or defixio.

EVERYDAY LIFE IN ANCIENT ROMAN TIMES
ROMAN RELIGION II - THE STATE GODS

The main Roman god was Jupiter. He was the Father of the state gods. His wife was Juno. The other important gods and goddesses are named in the family tree below. The Romans believed that each god and goddess looked after a particular aspect of their lives. For example, Mars was prayed to for success in war. Temples were built for these gods and were looked after by priests and priestesses.

FAMILY TREE OF THE ROMAN STATE GODS

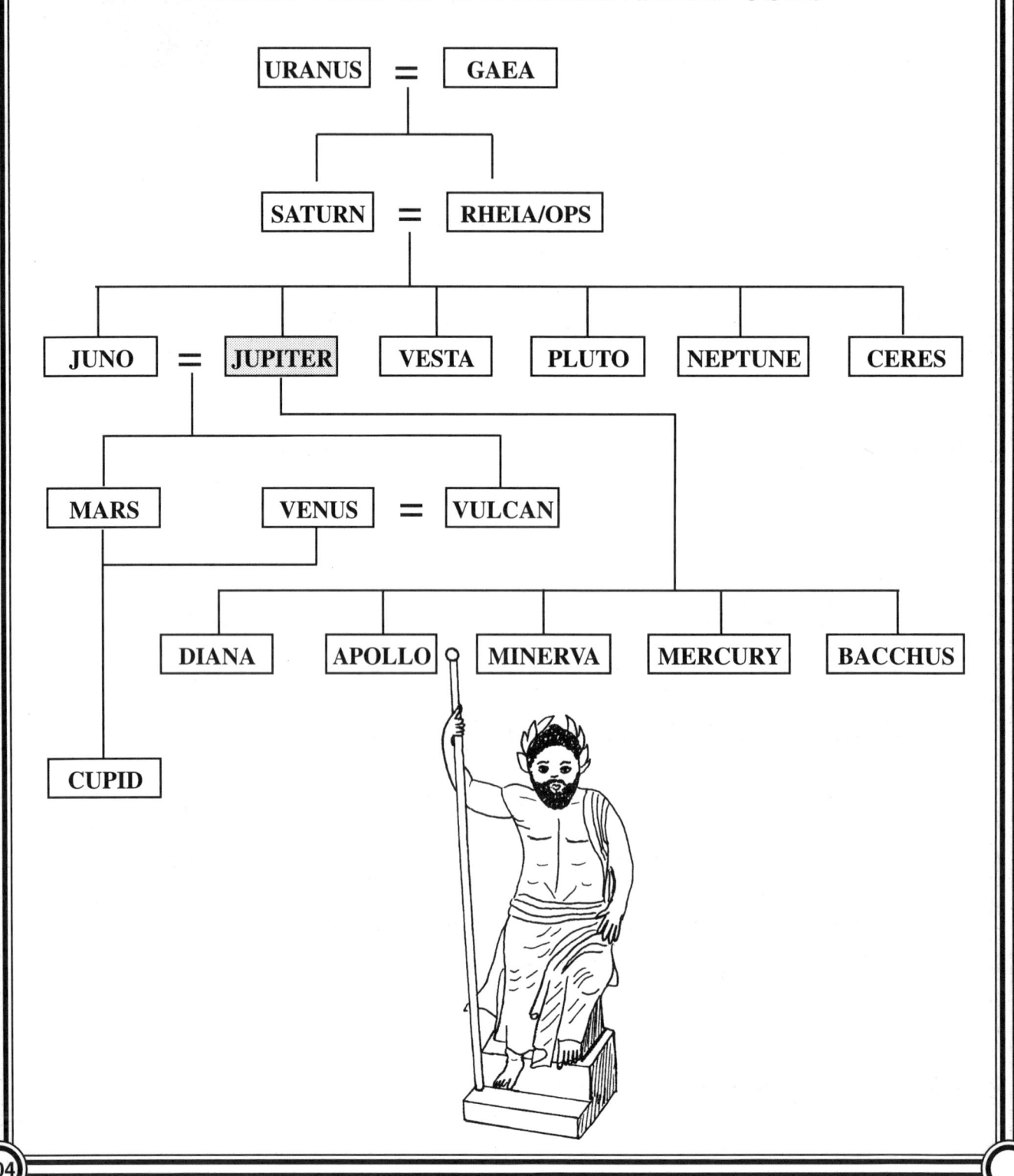

```
              URANUS = GAEA
                   |
              SATURN = RHEIA/OPS
                   |
   ┌──────┬────────┬────────┬────────┬────────┐
  JUNO = JUPITER  VESTA   PLUTO   NEPTUNE   CERES
       |
   ┌───┴───┐
  MARS   VENUS = VULCAN
   |        |
   |   ┌────┼────┬────────┬────────┐
   |  DIANA APOLLO MINERVA MERCURY BACCHUS
   |
  CUPID
```

EVERYDAY LIFE IN ANCIENT ROMAN TIMES

ROMAN RELIGION III

Look at the state gods' family tree carefully and answer these questions.

1. Jupiter's parents were: _____ and _____

2. How many brothers and sisters did Jupiter have and what were their names?
   _____

3. Which gods married their sisters? _____ , _____ and _____

4. Jupiter and Juno produced two sons together. Who were they?

   _____ and _____

5. Jupiter fathered five other children by different women. What were the names of these offspring?
   _____

6. What relation was Diana to Bacchus? _____

7. What relation was Apollo to Mercury? _____

8. What relation was Vulcan to Minerva? _____

9. Neptune was the _____ of Mars.

10. Saturn was the grandfather of which gods? _____
    _____

11. Who married Vulcan? _____

12. Who did Vulcan's wife mother a child with? _____

13. What was the name of Mars' son? _____

14. Apollo was Uranus' _____

15. Cupid was Jupiter's _____

EVERYDAY LIFE IN ANCIENT ROMAN TIMES

ROMAN RELIGION IV

Using a ruler and a colour, match the name of the gods and goddesses with what they were worshipped for.

JUPITER	Goddess of crafts and war
JUNO	God of fire and forges
APOLLO	Goddess of the hearth
MINERVA	God of wine
MARS	God of the underworld
MERCURY	Goddess of agriculture
VULCAN	Goddess of women
VENUS	God of the sea
NEPTUNE	Goddess of hunting & the moon
PLUTO OR DIS	God of war
VESTA	Goddess of love and beauty
CERES	God of trade, messenger of the gods
BACCHUS	God of music and the sun
DIANA	Father of the gods

SACRIFICES

Sacrifices of animals were made at an altar in front of the temple, to please the gods. The sacrifices were carried out by the chief priest, **pontifex maximus**, or the Emperor himself. He sprinkled the animal with salt, flour or wine. Part of the carcass was thrown onto the altar fire for the god to eat.

In the space below, draw the animals usually used for sacrifices:

Oxen   Sheep   Pigs   Goats   Doves

EVERYDAY LIFE IN ANCIENT ROMAN TIMES
ROMAN RELIGION V - OTHER GODS

As well as the state gods, the Romans believed that there were household gods too. They gave these gods gifts at an altar in their houses, and made sacrifices to them, in order to bring peace and happiness to the family. The **lares** were the spirits of the house, the **penates** were the spirits of the storeroom and **Janus** was the god of the doorway.

The Romans also adopted local gods, as their Empire enlarged: **Isis, Cybele** 'The Great Mother' and **Mithras** came from the East. The remains of a temple to Mithras were found in London. Local British gods, such as Brigantes, Nodens and Sul Minerva, were also adopted by the Romans.

Judaism was the chief religion in the Roman province of Judaea. The Jews were persecuted because of their belief in only one God and their refusal to worship the Roman gods. This led to the Romans destroying the Temple of Jerusalem in A.D. 70. This event is sculpted on the Arch of Titus in Rome.

Christianity was also an unpopular religion for the Romans and proved a threat to their own religion. Christians were told to love everyone, friends and enemies, and, if they led a good life they would be sent to Heaven after they died. The evil would go to Hell. Christians followed the teachings of Jesus of Nazareth, who taught them that there was only one God and not to worship the Roman gods. This angered the Roman governors of Judaea. However, the Emperor Constantine (A.D. 306-337) allowed Christians to worship freely, without persecution, and it became the main religion of the Roman Empire. Constantine himself became a Christian after seeing a vision in the sky. By A.D. 400, Christianity was the main religion in Roman Britain.

Did You Know?

Some Emperors became gods when they died and temples were built for them!

1. *Why did the Romans believe that it was important to worship the household gods?*

2. *Why did the Romans not tolerate either Judaism or Christianity?*

3. *Just before a battle, Emperor Constantine saw a cross in the sky and the words 'in hoc signo vinces', meaning 'you will conquer with this sign'. What do you think this meant for Constantine and for the Roman Empire?*

EVERYDAY LIFE IN ANCIENT ROMAN TIMES
ROMAN RELIGION VI - CHRISTIANITY

Christianity was becoming a popular religion in the Roman Empire, but many Romans believed that the Christians should also worship the state gods too. Christianity taught that there was only one God and that it was wrong to worship others, so many Christians refused to worship the Romans' gods. This caused great anger amongst the Roman officials, and many Christians were killed as a result.

Read the sources below and answer the questions:

Pliny has written to the Emperor Trajan telling him about how he deals with the problem of Christians:

> This is what I do to persons who think they might be Christians. I ask them if they are Christian and if they admit it, I repeat the question a second and a third time and warn them of the punishment that awaits them.
> If they persist, I order them to be led away and executed.
>
> PLINY letter to Emperor Trajan (100 A.D.)

The Emperor Trajan sends a reply to Pliny:

> These people must not be hunted out. If they are brought before you and they are guilty, they must be punished. If anyone denies that he is a Christian, and makes that clear by sacrifices to our gods, he is to be pardoned.
>
> EMPEROR TRAJAN letter to Pliny (100 A.D.)

1. *How could a Christian avoid being executed?*

2. *Why do you think that so many Christians refused to sacrifice to the Roman gods?*

EVERYDAY LIFE IN ANCIENT ROMAN TIMES
ROMAN RELIGION VII

These symbols were associated with the gods.

1. *Find out which symbol belongs to which Roman god or goddess. Write the name of the god or goddess beside it:*

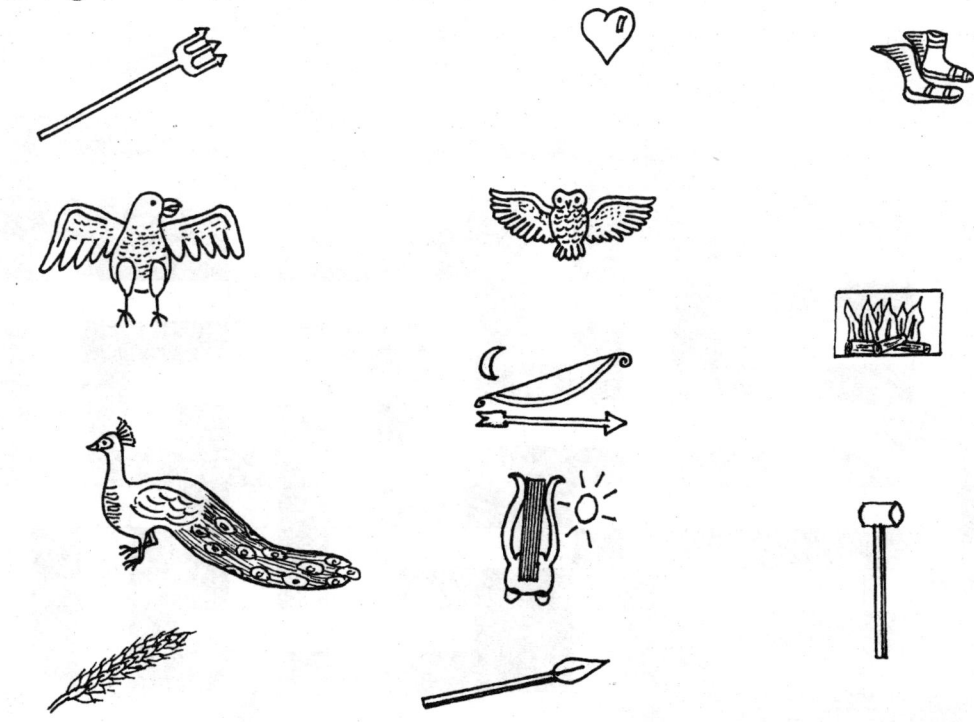

2. *In pairs or small groups, find out as much information as you can about one of the gods or goddesses listed below and write about them.*

Jupiter	Juno	Vesta	Neptune	Pluto
Ceres	Vulcan	Mars	Diana	Cybele
Bacchus	Apollo	Minerva	Mercury	Isis
	Venus	Mithras		

- Try to find a story or a myth about the god or goddess.
- Draw a large picture of the god or goddess you chose.

The Ancient Romans believed that the gods looked down on their lives.

3. *Write down as many things as you can think of, that the gods would find very different about religion if they looked down on our world today.*

EVERYDAY LIFE IN ANCIENT ROMAN TIMES

ROMAN RELIGION VIII

This crossword puzzle is about religion at the time of the Romans.
Use the clues below to help you to solve it.

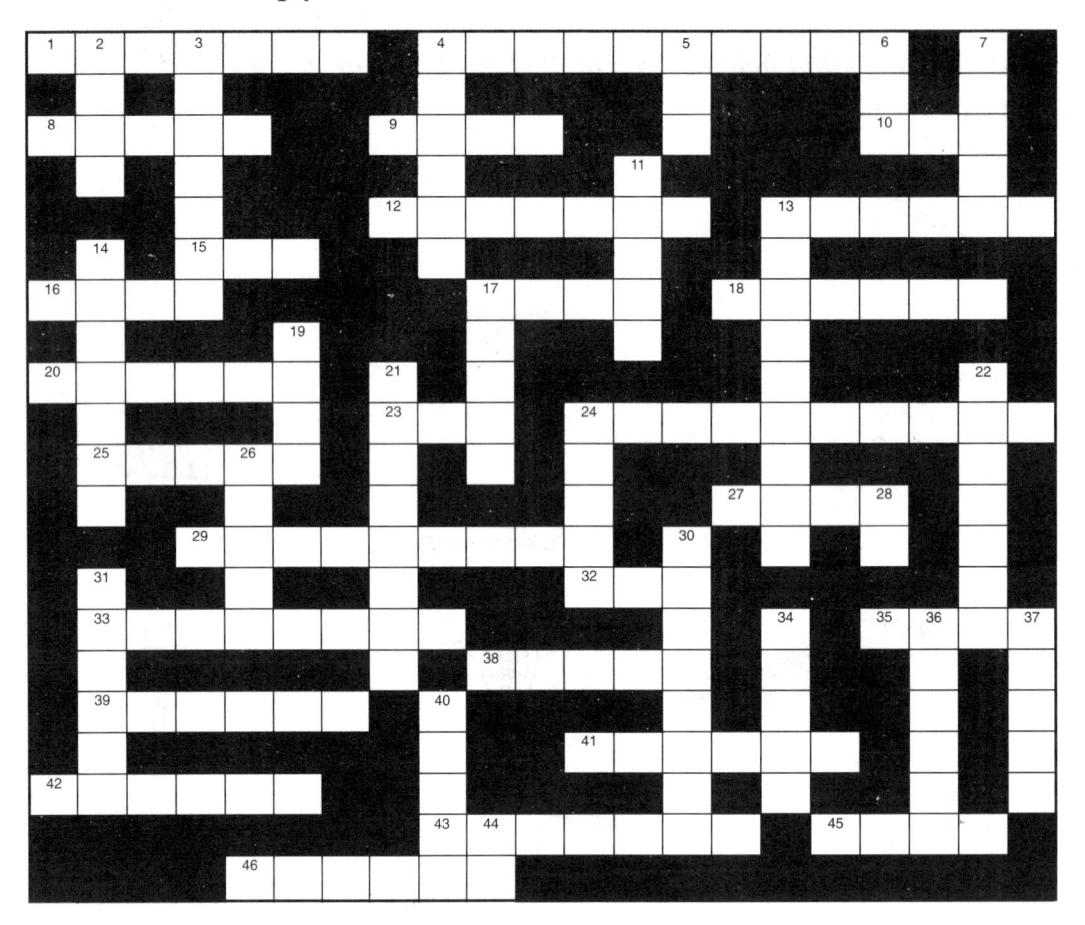

Across
1. This god came from Persia.
4. Where the Romans believed that they went after death.
8. This goddess is the sister of Minerva.
9. Vulcan's brother.
10. Apollo is the god of this.
12. He is the god of thunder and lightning & father of the gods.
13. Jesus . . . . was worshipped by Christians.
15. Romans tolerated and worshipped . . . gods.
16. Jesus was known as the . . . of the Jews.
17. Bacchus is the god of this.
18. Augurs looked at these to explain the mood of the gods.
20. Vesta is the goddess of this.
23. How many gods did the Christians believe in?
24. These people look at animal entrails to tell the future.
25. She is the goddess of the hearth.
27. Jupiter's wife.
29. This was made to please a god.
32. Neptune was the god of this.
33. These rulers became gods.
35. The wife of Uranus.
38. Minerva was the goddess of this.
39. Mithras came from here.
41. Jupiter sat on this.
42. Elysium, in the Underworld, was like the Christian . . .
43. Feminine form of a god.
45. Diana was the goddess of this.
46. Juno was the wife and . . . of Jupiter.

Down
2. Goddess of the East.
3. Diana is associated with this.
4. Jupiter's grandfather.
5. Minerva and Mars are both gods of this.
6. The god of the underworld.
7. This goddess married Vulcan.
11. Goddess of agriculture.
13. Large amphitheatre in Rome.
14. Goddess of craft and war.
17. Juno is the goddess of these people.
19. Wife of Saturn.
21. Mithras was worshipped by these people.
22. God of the sea.
24. Name of the underworld.
26. Mercury was the god of this.
28. An animal that was sacrificed to the gods.
30. 'Hell' of the underworld.
31. This building was built to honour a god.
34. These animals were used to kill Christians.
36. God of music.
37. A sacrifice to a god was made here.
40. Vulcan was the god of this.
44. A sheep . . . a dove may be sacrificed to a god.

EVERYDAY LIFE IN ANCIENT ROMAN TIMES

DEATH AND BURIAL

The Romans buried their dead in graves. Cemeteries were always outside the town walls, usually along the roads leading into the town. The dead body was carried in a procession to the cemetery. The family hired mourners and musicians who led the funeral procession. Sometimes a speech by a relative or a friend would be made in the forum to honour the dead person. There was a 'burial club' to which some Romans paid money. This then paid for their funeral.

DID YOU KNOW?
The Romans often buried their dead with food and drink so that they would not get hungry or thirsty in the next world. They also left money, favourite objects or games for them. Sometimes a coin was placed in the mouth of the dead person, to pay the ferryman Charon, to take their soul to the underworld.

The following were important to the Romans in death. In pairs or small groups, find out about the following:

Pluto, Dis or Hades
Proserpine
Hades (the place)
Tartarus
Elysium
River Styx
Charon the ferryman
Cerberus, the dog
Aeneas and his visit to the Underworld

Sisyphus, Tantalus and Tityos - were three men punished in Hades.
Find out what their punishments were.

Put your research together into a book about Roman death.

EVERYDAY LIFE IN ANCIENT ROMAN TIMES
DEATH AND BURIAL

The Romans had gravestones which were carved with names, numbers and messages. Usually these words were shortened or abbreviated:

DM	(dis manibus)	To the spirits of the dead
V or VIX	(vixit)	lived
AN	(annos/annorum)	years
D	(dies)	days
FILIUS		son
CIVIS		citizen
FC	(faciendum curavit)	had this made
PC	(ponendum curavit)	had this set up
HSE	(hic situs est)	is buried here
S	(sanctus)	sacred or holy
M	(miles)	soldier
HFC	(heres faciendum curavit)	the heir set this up
CONIUX PIETISSIMA		very loyal wife
LIBERA		freed woman
STIP	(stipendia - followed by numerals)	years a soldier spent in the army

Look at the gravestone below. Try to work out what it says and write it in English in the one beside it.

```
D M

FLAVIA DINYSIA

CONIUX
PIETISSIMA

VIX AN XL

HFC
```

HINT: The Roman woman's name is Flavia Dinysia!

THE COLLAPSE OF THE ROMAN EMPIRE

Illustrate the following events to make a timeline showing the collapse:

A.D. 330	Emperor Constantine builds a new city in the East (Constantinople).	
A.D. 340	The Picts attack Britain from the North.	
A.D. 367	Outer edges of the Empire face threats and attacks from tribes. E.g. Scotland. Picts, Scots and Saxons all attack Britain at the same time from different directions.	
A.D. 383	General Maximus (Roman) abandons Britain.	
A.D. 395	Roman army leaves Britain to fight in the rest of the Empire. Roman influence never leaves Britain completely.	

A.D. 409	Romans leave Britain in order to fight and defend the rest of Europe.	
A.D. 409	Civil War breaks out in Europe and attacks from barbarian tribes occur.	
A.D. 410	No Romans remain in Britain. However, the Roman influence never leaves Britain altogether.	
A.D. 410	Alaric and the Visigoths attack Rome. They kill Romans and enslave others. Buildings are burned.	
A.D. 455	Rome is attacked by a tribe called the Vandals.	
A.D. 476	Odoacer (a Goth) kills the last remaining Roman Emperor in the West. The City of Rome is reduced to ruins.	

WHAT HAS CHANGED AND WHAT HAS STAYED THE SAME?

Professor Oliver Strigil has invented a time machine that can help him to travel back to ancient Roman times!

Make a list, in the space below, of what he would find different from today. One has been done for you.

Clothes: The Ancient Romans wore togas. Modern Italians are fashion conscious and wear many designer outfits. However they do not resemble the toga!

What would he find the same as now? One has been done for you.

Buildings: Some modern buildings are built with Roman style columns.

EXTRA
You may like to make a poster of some of the differences or similarities that you have thought of.

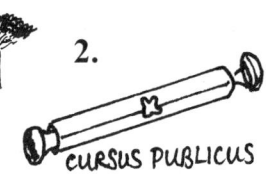

THE LEGACY OF ANCIENT ROME

Unscramble the words to reveal a number of things that the Romans have left us. Look carefully and see how many you can work out. Some of the pictures may help you! Write the words in the box provided.

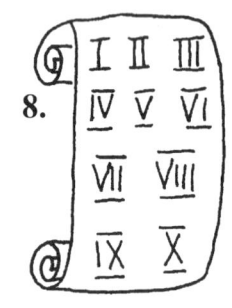

1.	1. DOARS
2.	2. LASTOP MESTYS
3.	3. LENACDER
4.	4. NUALGAGE
5.	5. STALF
6.	6. NOICS
7.	7. THANEGI
8.	8. SLAMERUN
9.	9. CHARES
10.	10. TELIOTS
11.	11. YIMFAL
12. **TOWNS**	12. WONTS

The Romans also left us with other ideas such as the idea of religion, laws, architecture and baths.

Using modern magazine pictures and your own illustrations etc. make a collage to show all the things that the Romans have left us.

'THE ROMANS' - Teachers' Notes

Who were the Romans? *Page 1*	In this worksheet, pupils are asked to think where they can learn and find out about the Romans. This activity forms a good introduction to learning about what history is. The aim is to introduce the idea of Primary and Secondary sources of evidence to pupils and is designed to instigate interesting discussion. 1. **PRIMARY** - evidence remaining from Roman times includes: - buildings, coins, letters, military records, writing, poems, plays, letters, weapons, inscriptions, sculptures, paintings, utensils, pots, tools etc. 2. **SECONDARY** - sources are from outside the time of the Romans and include: Video and TV programmes, taped stories, radio programmes, modern books, computers and CD ROMs about the Romans.
How to make a History Detective Wheel *Page 2*	Pupils can choose to make either a Primary or Secondary sources wheel or a combination of the two. The wheel is most effective if copied and enlarged onto A3 paper. Each circle can be mounted onto stiff paper or card. Pupils write the names of the sources on the outside edge of the larger circle and draw a picture, which can be viewed through the window on the smaller wheel when this is placed on top of the larger one. The two wheels should be attached to each other by the use of a split-pin, through the centres of the circles.
Roman Primary Sources I & II *Pages 3 & 4*	**Research skills:** This is a reinforcement activity for the previous pages. Pupils are asked to look for pictures of primary sources of evidence to draw or stick on the page. This activity could be carried out in groups or individually. A poster for a wall display could be created.
Archaeological Dig I & II *Pages 5 & 6*	**Research skills:** Pupils are asked to find out about archaeology and the job of an archaeologist. The activity teaches pupils an awareness of archaeology and its importance, the different tools required for uncovering evidence from the ground and their specific uses. A - a pick is used to loosen the earth. B - a trowel is used to remove layers of earth gently. C - a tape measure is used to measure the site and artefacts. D - a wheelbarrow is used to cart the soil away. E - a toothbrush is used to remove dirt from delicate objects. F - a spade is used to scoop the earth into the wheelbarrow. Pupils are asked to draw a simple conclusion from the archaeological evidence found. They should interpret that the artefacts found indicate the remains of a wealthy Roman woman. Pupils could continue this activity further through the invention of their own Roman remains. Ideas could include a Roman soldier or a Roman child. **Answers:** KLEENOTS - skeleton, PREMUFE TELBOT - perfume bottle, DOLG TRABECLE - gold bracelet, BREALM - marble, NIEW GUJ - wine jug, STIEL - tiles.

Roman Timeline I & II *Pages 7 & 8*	The aim of this activity is to place events accurately on to the timeline. Pupils should write the correct dates in the time sequence. They should be able to use the dates and vocabulary relating to the passing of time and understand why the dates go backwards (B.C.) They should understand the terms A.D. (*anno domini* - the year of Our Lord) & B.C. (the time *before Christ*). In order to place the period of ancient Rome in its historical context, a timeline of key events in history up to the present day can be made and displayed in the classroom. Pupils will then begin to understand the passing of time.
Where is Italy? *Page 9*	**Geographical Skills:** Pupils require an atlas for this activity to enable them to transfer information on to the map, in order to develop an understanding of the location of Rome and the main physical features around it. Reasons for its location as a settlement could be discussed and linked to the activities on pages 16 & 17. **Seven Hills of Rome:** PALATINE *(Mons Palatinus)*, CAPITOLINE *(Mons Capitolinus)*, AVENTINE *(Mons Aventinus)*, CAELIAN *(Mons Caelius)*, ESQUILINE *(Mons Esquilinus)*, VIMINAL *(Mons Viminalis)*, QUIRINAL *(Mons Quirinalis)*. **Seas:** MEDITERRANEAN *(Latin: Mare Internum)* TYRRHENIAN *(Latin: Mare Tyrrhenum)* ADRIATIC *(Latin: Mare Adriaticum)*. Also, the IONIAN and LIGURIAN seas lie to the southeast and northwest of Italy respectively. The Romans spoke Latin and travelled by boat, cart and horse on their road networks. **A comparison of Modern and Ancient Italy.** Group work works well for the research-based activities on *pages 10 & 11*. Divide the class into two groups, one for ancient and the other for modern Italy. Within these two groups, smaller groups can be established for the research. Written and oral presentations allow pupils to feed back to the rest of the class. The activities contrast the ancient and modern aspects of life and pupils should be asked to make comparisons, finding similarities and differences.

Where in the world is Modern Italy? *Page 10*	**Group Research using reference material** **Answers to questions:** 1. EUROPE 2. ROME 3. GREEN, WHITE, RED (vertical stripes) 4. MILAN, VENICE, FLORENCE, SIENA, NAPLES etc. 5. EURO (was the lira) 6. 57 / 58 million people 7. CAR INDUSTRY - Fiat, Ferrari, Lamborghini. FASHION INDUSTRY - clothing, leather, FOOD & WINE INDUSTRY. 8. ITALIAN 9. CLIMATE, HISTORY, CITIES, ART, MUSIC, CULTURE, FOOD, SPORT, SHOPPING 10. PASTA, PIZZA, SOUP, FRUIT, ICE-CREAM, OLIVES, WINE
Where in the world is Ancient Italy? *Page 11*	**Group Research using reference material** **Answers to questions:** 1. EUROPE. 2. ROMA in the country of ITALIA. 3. ROMULUS & REMUS (she-wolf suckling two babies). SPQR - *senatus populusque romanus* - The Roman Senate and People, inscribed at the base of statues. 4. POMPEII, HERCULANEUM, RAVENNA, OSTIA. 5. COINS - showed the head of the Emperor (AUREUS, DENARIUS, SESTERCII). 6. Rome's population was estimated to be between 450,000 and 750,000. 7. ROADS, TOILETS, ORGANISATION OF THE ARMY, TOWN PLANS, ARCHES, CALENDAR, NUMERALS 8. LATIN 9. Roman name for Mediterranean Sea - MARE INTERNUM, Britain - BRITANNIA, Spain - HISPANIA, France - GAUL OR GALLIA 10. FISH SAUCE, MEAT, NO POTATOES OR SUGAR. Romans used honey instead. It was very different from Italian food today.
The City of Rome *Page 12*	From this activity, pupils can learn about the history of Rome, to try and distinguish between legend and fact, and to establish why people in the past acted the way they did. Rome in the eighth century B.C. was originally a small tribal settlement on the Palatine hill near to the River Tiber. It was a suitable geographical settlement - near to water and with fertile land. With an increasing population, it expanded and developed its government and culture. It was taken over by the kingdom of Etruria, merging to become one city in 753 B.C., although modern historians have dated this to 625 B.C. The city was ruled over by seven Etruscan kings until 509 B.C. when the Romans finally took over. They established Rome as a republic (*res publica*) where its citizens elected a ruler or consul each year. From this time onwards, Rome's power increased and her Empire enlarged. The Romans adopted many Etruscan influences, such as their religion, their ideas and their civilisation.

Romulus and Remus *Pages 13 - 15*	In the first century B.C. two authors wrote about the legend of the origins and the founding of Rome - Virgil and Livy. Pupils need to be aware of the facts and the legend surrounding the foundation of Rome. They are asked to retell the story through illustration on the filmstrip pages. This will involve planning out what to include in each box. Discussion about the characters' actions can provide an insight into the period. **The legend:** Romulus and Remus, sons of the god Mars, were thought to be descended from the kings of Alba Longa, a city founded by Aeneas' son Ascanius. The story of Romulus and Remus may be based on some truth - two settlements around 8th century B.C. merged into one settlement. The statue of Romulus and Remus as babies, being suckled by the she-wolf, became an important symbol of Rome and many such statues still exist in Rome today.
Where would you have built a city like Rome? *Page 16 & 17*	**Geographical skills:** This activity involves looking at and giving reasons for the possible positioning of a settlement. They are expected to identify the natural geographical features in relation to Rome. In the sheets, pupils are asked to think of advantages and disadvantages of settling beside certain natural features. They are then asked to design their own map, drawing on more features, using a key and symbols and finally positioning their city in a suitable place on the map. They are asked to decide where they would choose to build a city and to justify their decision. This could lead to a debate in class followed by a piece of persuasive writing.
The Roman Emperors *Page 18*	**Historical Research, using reference materials.** The list of Emperors for research could be divided up between the members of the class. Pupils could be encouraged to display their work on the wall, in a book, as a poster etc. IMPERATOR - Latin for Emperor Official colour - Emperors wore purple Laurels - worn on head of Emperors as a symbol of their power. They did not wear crowns. **Background Information:** **Augustus** - Octavian became the first emperor in 27 B.C. and took the title of Augustus. He was the great-nephew and adopted son of Julius Caesar. He defeated Mark Antony and Cleopatra at the battle of Actium in 31 B.C. and he took charge, but to gain popularity, he based his rule on the traditions of the old republic. He brought peace and stability to Rome according to several authors - Suetonius, Livy and Virgil. Buildings in Rome were erected, including the Altar of Peace - *ara pacis,* indicating that it was a prosperous reign. He boasted that he found Rome in brick and left it in marble. He brought about changes, such as dividing Rome into 14 areas each controlled by a magistrate and introducing vigils, the first fire brigade. Emperors who followed him adopted the title *Augustus*, the dignified one. He died in A.D. 14.

Tiberius - Emperor from A.D. 14 - 37 and stepson of Octavian. He was an excellent administrator but he was not particularly popular. He was terrified of being assassinated so he retired to the island of Capri and ruled through his deputy Sejanus. Sejanus tried to seize power for himself but Tiberius had him executed. After this Tiberius became suspicious and a tyrant. Such was his paranoia that anyone who he thought opposed him was forced to commit suicide. Tacitus and Suetonius wrote the main contrasting sources for his reign. One is heavily biased towards him and the other writes scurrilous anecdotes about his life.

Caligula - Gaius was his name (Gaius Julius Caesar Germanicus) but he was nicknamed Caligula *(Little Boot)* because of the small soldier's boots *(caligae)* that he wore as a child. He ruled from A.D. 37 - 41. He grew up in various military camps by the River Rhine, where his father Germanicus was an officer. Suetonius describes him as cruel, extravagant and arrogant. He was generally believed to be mentally unbalanced. He is mainly remembered for giving a consulship to his own horse and for marrying his own sister. He ruled for four years and was murdered by the Praetorian Guard.

Claudius - (Tiberius Claudius Nero Germanicus) was emperor from A.D. 41 - 54. The army declared him Emperor following the death of his nephew Gaius (Caligula). He was weak and crippled, having a limp and a stammer, and most of his relatives thought that he was stupid and ridiculed him. He was in fact a very intelligent scholar - a good public speaker, an excellent historian who wrote several books, and a wise and sympathetic ruler. He was the first Emperor to make Britain a Roman province after his successful gain of the southeast. His wife Agrippina supposedly poisoned him. He was deified after his death.

Nero - (Nero Claudius Caesar) was emperor from A.D. 54 - 68. He was the last emperor of the Julio - Claudian line and was tutored by the philosopher Seneca. At first his rule was stable and effective but he soon became vain, arrogant and obsessed with power and jealous fears. Anyone who opposed him was murdered, including his own mother Agrippina. According to Suetonius, he sponsored public shows and games in which he appeared and he had to increase taxes to pay for them. Rumour spread that he caused the fire that destroyed much of Rome in A.D. 64 while he was said to have celebrated by playing his lyre and singing while watching the fire from his window. This is speculative. He began an organised persecution of Christians and blamed them for the fire. He eventually left Rome and was forced to commit suicide. His most famous building was his golden palace *(domus aurea)* in Rome, which was built on a most extravagant scale. A huge statue of himself as the sun god is said to have stood in the forecourt. Much of the palace is being excavated in Rome today.

Vespasian - (Titus Flavius Vespasianus) was emperor from A.D. 70 - 79. He came to power after the death of Nero and the short rules of Galba, Otho and Vitellius. He restored order to Rome and stability to the empire, making improvements in the administration and the army. He began major public building works in Rome, including the Colosseum, temples and restorations to the forum.

Trajan - (Marcus Ulpius Trajanus) was emperor from A.D. 98-117, succeeding the Emperor Nerva. He was born in Spain and was an outstanding soldier and general. His military successes are sculpted spirally on a large column in Rome known as Trajan's Column. The empire grew to its largest under his reign and he conquered Dacia and Parthia. He built baths, markets, a basilica and a new forum in Rome and he was given the title of *Optimus Princeps* (Best Prince), which appears on his coins and monuments.

Hadrian - (Publius Aelius Hadrianus) was emperor from A.D. 117-138. He came from a distinguished family in Spain. He succeeded his relative and adoptive father Trajan. He was a great soldier and spent much of his rule with the armies in the provinces. Unlike Trajan, he set up barriers on the edges of the empire to keep out the barbarians rather than expand the empire further. Hadrian's wall in Britain is an example of this. He was a patron of the arts and a scholar, who built a library in Athens and a villa for himself at Tivoli near Rome. Around A.D. 135 he set up an organisation called the Athenaeum to sponsor writers and philosophers and wrote poetry himself. He was buried in a large tomb that he had designed for himself in Rome. Subsequent emperors were also buried there.

Septimius Severus - (Lucius Septimius Severus) was emperor from AD 193-211. He was born in Lepcis Magna in North Africa. He was responsible for the sea port built there. He defeated the Parthians and an arch in Rome commemorates his victories. He was a military man but he was a good ruler of the civil population. One of his achievements was to reconstruct Hadrian's wall in stone. However, he is also remembered for riding over the dead body of his opponent Clodius Albinus intentionally.

Diocletian - was emperor from A.D. 284-305. He was declared emperor by his troops. He made many reforms to coinage, taxation, the army and the organisation of the empire. He split the empire into two parts, ruling the east himself and appointing the emperor Maximian to rule the west. His administrative systems lasted for centuries.

Constantine - (Flavius Valerius Constantinus) was emperor from A.D. 306-337 following his father Constantius' death. He defeated his rival Maxentius for the throne, in a battle at the Milvian Bridge. This is remembered on the Arch of Constantine in Rome. It was before this battle that Constantine was said to have had a vision of the Cross. He moved the imperial court and capital of the empire from Rome to a new city on the Black Sea, which he called Constantinople (now Istanbul). Constantine was the first Christian emperor and ruled as sole emperor from AD 323. He tried to unite the divided Empire. He granted freedom of worship to Christians through the Edict of Milan in AD 313 but also tolerated the pagans. He was baptised a Christian on his deathbed.

Julian - (Flavius Claudius Julianus) was emperor from A.D. 360-363. On becoming emperor he began to restore the worship of the ancient pagan Roman gods, going against Christianity, which was now the official religion of the state. He was known as *Julian the Apostate* because he abandoned Christianity for the Roman religion. He improved the civil service but was unpopular because of his religious views. Some of his letters and other writings survive and give us details of that time.

CELTIC BRITAIN
A study of Britain at the time of the Romans

Celtic Britain

Pages 19 - 32

The sheets on Celtic Britain can be used as a mini-study in a project on the Romans. They form an introduction and set the background to the study of Britain at the time of the Romans. The sheets can be used in different ways: pupils can collect information from them for an individual or group project, or they could simply work through the activities on the sheets. The sheets can also be used to compare aspects of life of the Romans and Celts, using the *Everyday Life in Roman Times* photocopiable sheets from this pack. Comparisons can also be drawn between this period of history and modern society.

The Roman sources generally painted the Celts in a bad light - as blue-painted savages whose only quality was bravery. However, some aspects of Celtic life were very advanced, such as their metal work and their agricultural systems. It was an oral culture and Celtic written evidence is very scarce.

Photocopiable sheets include a title page and worksheets on the following:

I - Who were the Celts? - The tribal system is explained in this sheet. Each tribe had its own ruler or chief and this contrasts with the Roman way of life.

Pupils can work out which tribe they would have belonged to by using the map.

II - Religion - This sheet can be used in drawing comparisons between the Roman and Celtic religions. Superstition seems to be an important link between the religions and neither religion was monotheistic. Foretelling the future is an important aspect of both religions as was sacrificing animals to placate the gods.

Photocopiable sheet - *page 103* could be used to draw further comparisons.

III - Festivals - a brief look at the kind of festivals that the Celts celebrated.

IV - Clothing - comparisons can be drawn between Celtic clothing and Roman clothing - see *pages 91-93*. Pupils are asked to follow instructions to make their own Celtic Brooch.

V - Women - this sheet draws comparisons between Roman and Celtic women and could act as a planning page for a wall display, or pupils could re-enact a discussion between two women. The photocopiable sheet *(page 86)* may also be helpful. The main difference is that Celtic women could have so much power in the tribe, even becoming leaders. Roman women had to obey the *paterfamilias* or father of the house and could not be decision makers except in the household.

VI - Produce - this sheet shows how the Celts survived and how skilled they were in producing their own equipment and food.

VII - Celtic Pot - pupils are asked to make their own Celtic pot.

VIII - Warfare - Celtic warriors were aggressive people and the clothing that they wore, as well as the way they fought, contrasted strongly with the orderly ranks of the Roman Army. They used bronze and iron weapons, which were highly decorated. They rode in chariots but fought on foot. They wore no body armour but their own clothes. They dyed their bodies and faces to look ferocious and blew a horn when charging into battle, to try to frighten their opponents. They had no order when attacking the Romans and seemed like an unruly mob. The organised Roman soldiers usually defeated them.

The Romans were divided into sections. They were very organised and marched in columns. They wore armour and the army consisted of a large number of men. They would have looked very formidable. Both the Romans and the Celts built forts and strong defences.

Pupils are asked to read the two quotes from Caesar and Suetonius, two Roman authors, to work out what these Romans thought of the Celtic Warriors. These sources could lead to an interesting discussion about opinions of others and bias.

The Roman Army sheets *(pages 36 & 37)* could be used to draw comparisons between the Celts and Romans.

IX to XIII - Houses - pupils learn about the way that the Celts lived and the different styles of houses that they lived in. They are asked to draw comparisons between them and to think about the advantages and disadvantages of each.

The property advertisement is an opportunity for pupils to write for a particular purpose. The examples demonstrate the type of language and expressions used. Newspaper advertisements and property leaflets could also be used as examples.

Pupils can make comparisons between Celtic and Roman houses, by using these sheets and *pages 75 & 77.*

THE ROMAN ARMY

These sheets can be used for research for a mini-project or pupils can work through the sheets as part of a study on the Roman Army.

Weapons and Equipment *Pages 33 & 34*	**Reading for Information:** Pupils use and reorganise the information on *page 34* to label the diagram on *page 33*. **Background Information:** A great deal is known about the armour worn by Roman soldiers and the weapons that they carried from sculptures and archaeological digs. Romans were issued with a short stabbing sword, a dagger and two javelins. Every soldier joining the army received a uniform and the cost of it was deducted from his pay. A soldier also carried tools for building roads and forts as well as his own personal possessions. Any losses had to be paid for out of his own wages.
Long-range weapons *Page 35*	Many of the long-range weapons came from Greek designs, but were refined by the Romans to suit their purposes. **Research** - pupils could research the different types of long-range weapons - the catapult, the onager and the ballista in groups. • **The onager** (translated as *wild ass* because of its kicking action) was a giant catapult, which hurled large and heavy boulders up to 500 metres. • **The ballista** was a weapon used to fire arrows and metal bolts up to 300 metres. It was designed to fire a succession of arrows. The practical test to compare the distance of an onager and a ball thrown demonstrates the strength of the weapons made by the Romans. This sheet links with the Technology Sheet III where pupils are asked to make a long-range weapon.
Organisation of the army *Pages 36 & 37*	The two sheets comparing Celtic Warriors and Roman Soldiers also link with *page 27*. Pupils are asked to interpret which kind of soldier they would prefer to be, based on the information given on the sheets, and should be encouraged to justify their opinions. **Background Information:** The Celts were aggressive warriors. They used bronze and iron weapons, which were highly decorated. They rode in chariots but fought on foot. They wore no body armour but their own clothes. They dyed their bodies and faces to look ferocious. The Roman soldiers were divided into 28 sections called *legions,* each with around 5,000 - 6,000 men. Each legion was again divided into smaller groups: a *century* made up of 80 men (originally 100) down to a small group of eight soldiers called a *contubernium* who shared a tent and who ate together. A century was led by a *centurion* and an *optio*. Centuries grouped together to form cohorts. Each legion was made up of 10 cohorts, the first cohort having 10 centuries or 800 men. The other nine had 6 centuries or 480 men. Legions were made up of soldiers, clerks, doctors, priests, engineers, surveyors and auxiliaries. The legion was under the command of the *legatus*. Under him were officers called *tribunes* or *tribuni*. The army was very organised and consisted of a large number of men who marched in columns. All soldiers wore uniform and carried their weapons. They would have looked very formidable to the Celts.

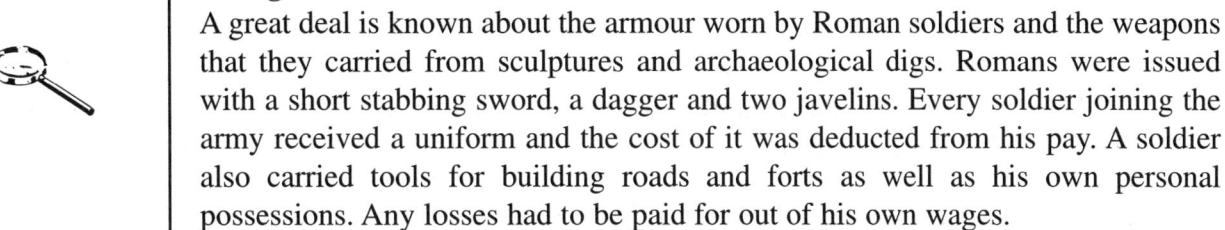

Army Research *Pages 38 & 40*	**Historical Research** - this sheet should be used with the information on *page 40 - Life as a Roman Soldier.* The questions help to give a structure to the research. These sheets work well as a group activity. Groups could present and display their work in a number of different ways - for example, as a poster or a handbook. The Romans were able to expand their empire as far as they did because of the strength of the army. It was the first paid full-time army and was very efficient. It was so powerful that it could defeat other armies larger than itself.
Life as a Roman Soldier in the Army *Pages 39 & 40*	The activity on *page 39* can be used as a brainstorming sheet. Pupils are asked to think of ideas of what equipment a soldier would need to take with them on a campaign. Following this activity, pupils should be given *page 40* to see what the soldiers actually took and needed, and to compare this with their own ideas. A good follow-up activity is the writing of a soldier's handbook, so that the information in the text can be interpreted and applied, but in a creative way. **Why do you think the Roman soldiers had heavier shields and swords for training?** In order to make the soldiers stronger so that their real weapons used in campaigns seemed easier to wield. As a result, the soldiers were able to fight for longer. **Background Information:** Life in the army was tough. Legionary soldiers were Roman citizens aged between 25 and 50 who had to be very fit. They trained by running, chopping trees, building and climbing. Three times every month they had to do an 18 mile route march with very heavy equipment, weapons and armour to carry. They had to march at a constant pace and this made them extremely strong. They were drilled and trained to use their weapons efficiently. **Discipline:** The centurions were in charge of discipline. They regularly beat the soldiers with a hardwood stick. Soldiers were given extra duties, fined, deprived of rations or flogged if caught doing something wrong. Serious crimes were punished by *decimation,* which was when the centurion touched every tenth man in the lines, and these men were killed by stoning. The term 'to decimate' comes from this. At the end of their service, Roman soldiers were given a pension and some land. Any foreigner who had served loyally in the army was made a citizen and slaves could be freed.
The Roman Army IX - British Forts *Page 41*	**Geographical skills:** A geographical activity, plotting the key fort bases in Britain, showing the extent of the Roman Invasion and the two boundaries. Pupils will need to use an atlas to position the places accurately.

Roman Army Technology *Pages 42, 43 & 44*	**Technology activities include:** design of a military standard making of a Roman soldier (using the template provided) making a model ballista Pupils can explore the design process (planning, designing, making, evaluating and modifying / altering) using these technology ideas. The activities work well as group projects or individually.
Julius Caesar *Pages 45, 46 & 47*	The primary sources on *pages 45 & 46* are written by Caesar himself and so involve his own version of events. Pupils should be encouraged to analyse the use of his writing and determine how reliable it is as evidence of what really happened. For example, he claimed that his invasion of Britain was *to teach the British a lesson* for helping the Gauls, but it is believed that it was more to impress the people of Rome and to outshine his opponents. Caesar described the difficulties that he faced in Britain so that his achievements were more impressive. **Historical Research, using reference materials.** People had different opinions about Julius Caesar. The research on *pages 46 & 47* is designed to enable pupils to find out as much as they can about Julius Caesar and to draw their own conclusions and opinions of him. **Background Information:** Julius Caesar was born in 100 BC. He was a famous politician and a great soldier and was the first Roman to lead an army against the Britons. He wanted to teach them a lesson as they had supported his enemies in Gaul. His first invasion did not meet with success in the long term, apart from capturing a few hostages, but his second invasion was more successful and the Romans conquered a small part of Britain. This time his army covered about 94 miles and defeated Cassivellaunus, a tribal leader. Caesar however soon retreated to Gaul again. Caesar made some important changes. He created a new calendar on which our calendar today is based - see *page 89 - Latin Language*, and he started a daily newspaper. He became the most powerful man and the sole leader and this led to unease in the Senate. A group of senators, including Brutus and Cassius, plotted to kill him in order to regain their power. Caesar was stabbed to death in the Senate on 15th March 44 B.C. This date is still known as the *Ides of March*. The month of July in our calendar is named after him. Shakespeare wrote a play called *Julius Caesar*.
Claudius' Invasion of Britain *Pages 48 & 49*	This activity explores the motives and actions of the Emperor Claudius and the effect that his motives had on his popularity. The activity on *page 49* allows pupils to place the statements in order of importance. This acts as a springboard for discussion about differences of opinion as not everyone will have put them in the same order. **Background Information:** Emperor Claudius was a wise ruler who ordered an invasion of the southeast of Britain in A.D. 43. It was led by Aulus Plautius, who became the first governor. He invaded out of fear of his army rising up and turning against him as he was becoming more unpopular. There was also general unease and discontentment in Rome following the murder of his predecessor (Caligula). Britain became a Roman province for the first time because the soldiers stayed.

Boudicca *Pages 50, 51 & 52*	In this activity, pupils are asked to write a diary for each stage of Boudicca's fight with the Romans. Activity sheet 1 can be used for information and a plan has also been included to provide a structure. *Page 52* - pupils can use the primary source written by Cassius Dio describing Boudicca in order to draw her. Discussion about Dio's description should be encouraged. Is it a true likeness of the Celtic queen or may he be exaggerating for effect? All the main sources for Boudicca's invasion are Roman. **Background Information:** Boudicca belonged to the Trinovantes tribe and she married Prasutagus, the King of the Iceni, an ancient tribe from what is now Norfolk, thus becoming queen. When the king died, he left half his kingdom to the Roman Emperor, hoping his wife and daughters would keep the rest. It did not work. The Romans tried to take over the whole kingdom and treated the queen and her daughters badly. It was because of this that the Iceni people, led by Boudicca, rose up against the Romans. They attacked Camulodunum (Colchester), battering down temple doors, hacking men, women and children to death and setting fire to the town before leaving. They killed anyone they could find in Londinium (London) too, throwing the bodies into the river. She next destroyed Verulamium (St Albans). All three of the largest towns in Britain were destroyed and she killed about 60 - 70 000 people. A fight between the Iceni army (100 000 men, women and children) and the Roman Army (10 000 soldiers) took place. The Roman Army killed 80 000 Iceni and only lost 400 of their own soldiers. Boudicca escaped rather than be taken prisoner and poisoned herself.
The Walls of Hadrian and Antoninus Pius *Pages 53 - 56*	The activities on these pages allow pupils to study and research the two Roman boundaries in Britain and to understand why the Romans needed these defences. Hadrian's wall was built earlier and was a strong defence against the Northern tribes. It had a number of features, such as a ditch, milecastles, forts etc. Hadrian himself visited Britannia in A.D. 122 and ordered the wall to be built by the legionary soldiers. Much information is available today about the wall and the research activity allows pupils to collect as much information as possible, to make a guidebook. They could construct a book similar to the one on *page 99*. There are far fewer remains of the Antonine Wall in Scotland because it only had a stone base. The rest of it consisted of turf blocks and wood. It was between 37 and 40 miles long and was built in about A.D. 142 under the reign of Emperor Antoninus Pius. It had 19 forts along its wall. Some remains exist in Bearsden but many of the stone slabs remain buried. The sequencing activity is devised to create discussion. There are no set answers in this activity. The technology pages allow pupils to build a simple 3D Roman fort like the ones built along Hadrian's wall. It looks particularly effective when painted. It may be better and easier to do this before finally constructing and gluing it together.
Roman Britain Timeline *Page 57*	The list shows the key events in Roman Britain. Pupils could devise and create a timeline for the wall as an extension activity, illustrating these important dates. Roman occupation of Britain lasted about 400 years. They should be able to use the dates and vocabulary relating to the passing of time and understand why the dates go backwards (B.C.). They should understand the terms A.D. (*anno domini* - the year of Our Lord) & B.C. (the time *before Christ*).

Growth of the Roman Empire and Roman Britain *Pages 58 & 59*	The first two maps show the growth of the Roman Empire under Julius Caesar and how it had spread by the time Hadrian was Emperor. They develop the concept of what an empire is and of its extent. It was the Emperor Claudius who originally made Britain a Roman province. Comparisons can also be drawn from the two maps of Britain, comparing the invasions of the Emperor Hadrian and the Emperor Antoninus Pius.
Roman Roads *Pages 60 & 61*	One of the important legacies left by the Romans was their road network, which ran to every corner of the empire - hence the expression 'all roads lead to Rome'. They were well built with proper foundations and allowed people to move around more easily. Soldiers could defend the province more effectively with good roads as they allowed for swift movement, communication was faster and roads helped merchants to sell their wares in more places. Therefore trade prospered. Pupils are asked to brainstorm why they thought roads were important. *Page 61* asks questions based on the information from *page 60*.
Roman Roads in Britain *Pages 62, 63 & 64*	**Geographical research:** Here pupils are asked to investigate and try to find any remains of Roman roads in their local area. The use of a good Ordnance Survey map will help them to discover if these roads ran between towns or forts. On a broader spectrum and looking at the whole of Britain, this activity allows pupils to discover which places have names derived from Latin. This works well as a fun group exercise. An ODOMETER was a machine invented originally by the Greeks but was adopted by the Romans. It was attached to the wheel of a carriage and it measured the number of rotations of the carriage wheel and thus the distance travelled. It is similar to a mileometer used in a modern car today. *Page 63* shows the network of roads built in Britain by the Romans. The activity allows pupils to research if these roads are still used today. Pupils are asked to record their findings of four different roads in the table on *page 64*.
Roman Towns in Britain *Pages 65 - 69*	**Geographical skills:** **Roman Towns in Britain I** This activity enables pupils to focus on a specific town in Britain and to look at it as a settlement. They are asked to observe, from the use of maps, whether there are any natural features near by (such as rivers, sea, hills etc.) and to mark these on their sketch map. Taking these features into account, they are then asked to draw conclusions as to why this particular site was important and was chosen by the Romans. Good examples of Roman towns in Britain include Vindolanda (near to Hadrian's wall), Corbridge, Wroxeter, Bath, Chester, York, Thetford and Silchester. **Roman Towns in Britain II, III & IV** Here pupils are asked to match the Roman town with the equivalent modern British town. **Answers:** EBORACUM - York DEVA - Chester VIROCONIUM CORNOVIORUM - Wroxeter

GLEVUM - Gloucester
ISLA DUMNONIORUM - Exeter
LINDUM - Lincoln
LONDINIUM - London
DUROBRIVAE - Rochester
AQUAE SULIS - Bath
VERULAMIUM - St Albans
CORINIUM - Cirencester
CAMULODUNUM - Colchester

Roman Towns in Britain III & IV

The Romans built towns in all their provinces. Each town was built to an orderly and organised plan, with streets laid out in straight lines, crossing each other at right angles. There would usually be two main streets that divided the town and smaller streets led off them. The streets were crowded and dirty - with rubbish and sewage. There were road sweepers (*curatores viarum*) who cleaned the streets and removed rubbish. They tended to be slaves.

Page 67 - this sheet gives information about the typical structure of a Roman town and shows the key buildings. The activity on *pages 68 and 69* allows pupils to make a Roman town plan. They are asked to cut out the pictures carefully and stick them in the correct place on the grid, using the co-ordinates.

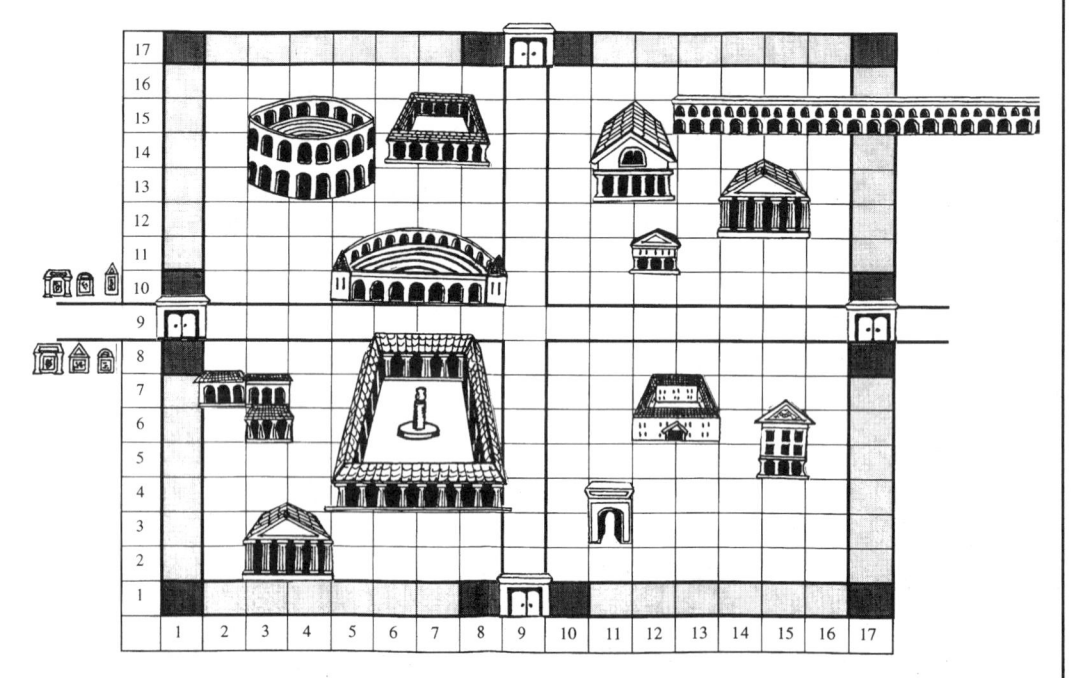

Pupils can be asked to draw comparisons between the layout of a modern town centre with that of a Roman town. This should involve looking at modern town plans and maps. What features, if any, are similar and what are the main differences?

Background Information

Forum - A town square where important government buildings were built (law courts and offices). There were also market and food stalls. It was the centre of the town and was where most business was conducted.

Thermae - The bath houses were for washing and were also places for socialising with friends. They were similar to our modern leisure centres. However men and women attended at different times. They were composed of hot and cold pools. There were also food stalls and exercise areas.

Amphitheatre - Shows were put on in amphitheatres - gladiators fighting each other or wild animals attacking/killing people.

Basilica - This was in the centre of the town and was like a town hall, containing law courts and government offices.

Temples - Here the Romans worshipped their gods. The Romans often adopted the local gods and sometimes the Emperors became gods after they died.

Insulae - Most people lived in blocks of flats which were several storeys high, the poorer living on the highest floors in the block. The rich lived in a domus or house.

Aqueducts - Water was carried to towns from the countryside via aqueducts, which were large bridges composed of a number of arches. Pipes and sewers took waste away.

Town Gate - Towns were built and surrounded by walls. Gates let people and animals into and out of the town. Graveyards were set up outside the town walls, along the roads leading into the town.

The Roman Toilet
Page 70

This activity compares how a way of life has changed and how it has stayed the same. Archaeological evidence has allowed us to discover different customs - for example, fragments of sponge have been found in the drains and sewers, confirming that the Romans used sponges on sticks to clean themselves.

The Romans built good water drainage systems in their towns. In the city of Rome there were seven sewers underground, which emptied into the River Tiber. They invented flushing toilets, but their toilets were very different from our modern ones. The sheet explains the main differences and similarities.

Pupils are asked to write a short and fun imaginative piece, as if they were a Roman visiting our time and experiencing our modern toilets. The individual cubicles in public toilets would surprise them and the concept of toilet paper would puzzle them.

The City of Rome
Page 71

This sheet outlines some important buildings and monuments from Roman times that still exist in Rome today. Pupils are asked to match the label to the building.

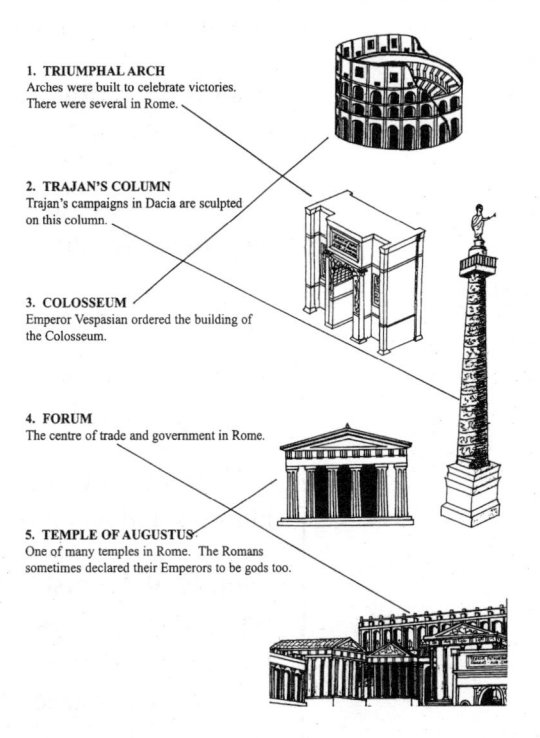

1. **TRIUMPHAL ARCH**
Arches were built to celebrate victories. There were several in Rome.

2. **TRAJAN'S COLUMN**
Trajan's campaigns in Dacia are sculpted on this column.

3. **COLOSSEUM**
Emperor Vespasian ordered the building of the Colosseum.

4. **FORUM**
The centre of trade and government in Rome.

5. **TEMPLE OF AUGUSTUS**
One of many temples in Rome. The Romans sometimes declared their Emperors to be gods too.

Triumphal Arches were built by emperors to celebrate and commemorate their victories. Some were quite plain but others had elaborate marble carvings, depicting the scenes from the battle won.

Trajan's Column. The emperor Trajan had a marble column (about 38 metres high) built in Rome to celebrate his victories in Dacia. The campaigns are sculpted on the column. The column is cleverly built and as it gets higher, the width increases, so that it doesn't look as though it narrows at the top. The base of the column supposedly contains a golden urn containing the ashes of the Emperor Trajan and his wife. They were the only Romans buried inside the city walls.

Colosseum - was a large stone amphitheatre (circumference 527m, height 57m) originally called the Flavian Amphitheatre as it was built under the reigns of the Flavian emperors. It became known as the Colosseum when Hadrian moved a statue of Nero, known as the *Colossus,* beside it. It could seat up to 50 000 spectators and was divided into three parts:- the *arena*, the *podium* and the *cavea*. The circular *arena* is named after *harena* (sand) which covered the central floor. This is where the spectacle took place. Underneath the *arena* floor were many passageways where cages and scenery were kept. The *podium* was a terrace on top of the arena wall where important people such as the Emperor or senators sat. They had the best view. The *cavea* was where the crowds sat. It was divided into three tiers, reached by stairs. Only men were allowed to sit in the bottom two tiers and women were separated and could only occupy the top tier. The building was enormous but could be emptied within ten minutes due the large number of arched entrances and exits.

Forum - was a place in the centre of the city or town where many government offices and official buildings such as the senate house *(curia)*, temple and law courts *(basilica)* were built. Political discussions took place and speeches were made there, and Romans also traded in the markets and shops there.

There were several *fora* built in Rome under different Emperors. Each one joined on to the original Roman Forum.

The Roman Forum was the original forum but was small and could not hold the crowds who gathered there.

Imperial Forum. Julius Caesar built this in 51 B.C. In order to make room for it, Caesar ordered the destruction of an entire street of houses which were in the way. It was estimated to have cost between 60 and 100 million sestertii. It was partially damaged by fire in A.D. 80 but was later restored. A temple to Venus Genetrix was built in the forum because Caesar claimed he was descended from the goddess.

Augustus' Forum contained the Temple of Mars Ultor.

Vespasian's Forum was known as the Peace Forum and a Temple of Peace was built there in A.D. 71 after the Jews were defeated in Judea.

Trajan's Forum was built next to his market and housed a basilica, a temple, two libraries and his famous column.

Temple of Augustus was one of an enormous number of temples in the fora and city of Rome. There were temples to the gods and goddesses as well as deified Emperors such as Augustus and Vespasian. Augustus built a temple to Julius Caesar on the place where his body was cremated.

Roman Architecture I, II & III

Pages 72, 73 & 74

This is an activity intended to teach pupils to be able to identify columns and capitals still used and existing in architecture today.

Background Information:
The Romans borrowed many architectural ideas and designs from the Greeks. However, the Romans' main interest in architecture was a practical one rather than decorative - the need for aqueducts to carry large amounts of water, bridges to cross large rivers like the Rhine and Danube and the need for enormous buildings, such as amphitheatres, for entertainment. The Romans were good engineers and they developed arches, vaults and domes which could span a large distance.

Columns and Capitals
The Romans copied the Greeks with their use of columns in architecture. They adopted the Ionic, Doric and Corinthian capitals and created the Composite (a combination of the Corinthian and Ionic) and Tuscan capitals.

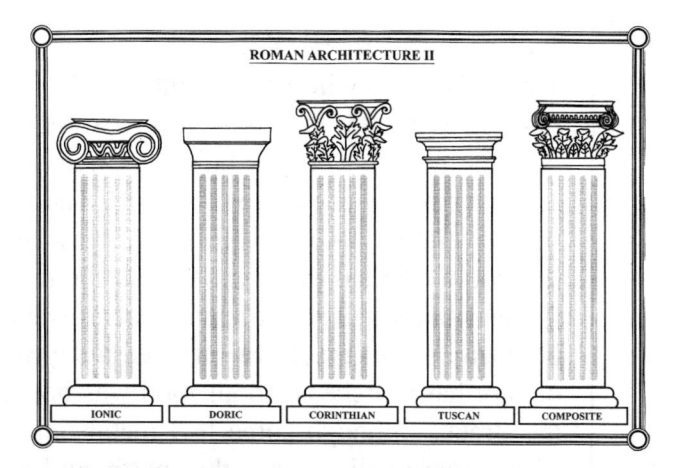

ROMAN ARCHITECTURE II

IONIC · DORIC · CORINTHIAN · TUSCAN · COMPOSITE

The **Pantheon** is a large building in Rome. It was built under the rule of Hadrian and was known as the 'Temple to all the gods'. The entrance *portico* resembled a typical temple, with columns, but inside, it had the largest domed ceiling in existence. An *oculus* (circular opening) in the roof let the sunlight stream in.

EVERYDAY LIFE IN ANCIENT ROMAN TIMES

The worksheets in this section can be used as they stand or used as a reference springboard for group research, dividing the topics between the groups. The information that pupils collect can be presented in a number of different ways - as talks, mini books or guides, and posters etc. and they make attractive displays. The activities enable pupils to draw comparisons between the ancient and modern elements of life.

Roman Houses

Pages 75 & 76

In this activity, direct comparison can be made between our houses today and those of the Ancient Romans. Pupils are asked to draw a plan of their own home and to label each room with its Latin name. Of course, some rooms that we have today will not have existed in Roman houses and vice versa. The activity asks for these to be listed.

Background Information:
The city of Rome in the 4th century A.D. had almost 50 000 *insulae* or blocks of flats. The greatest threats were thefts and fires (from oil-burning lamps used to light the home), as upper buildings were made of wood. The Emperor Augustus set up a fire brigade to combat fires. The flats differed in size - some were large with several rooms while others had only one room. The poor tended to live on the top floors whereas the rich lived on the lower floors, which were made of stone. Romans had small rugs but no carpets. Their furniture tended to be made of wood but many pieces that have survived today were made from marble or metal. Flats did not have kitchens, so all food was bought from snack bars and food stalls in the streets, although some had metal braziers which burned wood or charcoal. Slaves carried all water to the apartment blocks from a local fountain.

The rich lived in a *domus* or town house. There were only about 2 000 of these in the city of Rome. They had a number of rooms and tended to have running water and sometimes bathrooms. They also had large kitchens with different fires for cooking different types of food.

Central Heating

Page 77

Pupils are asked to think about advantages and disadvantages of the Roman heating system and to draw comparisons with their heating systems at home.

Background Information:
The Romans invented the *hypocaust* or central heating system in about 85 B.C. It was the first under-floor central heating system. Slaves stoked the fires usually with wood, which heated the rooms. The hot air rose up and flowed through gaps between the walls and under the floors. The room could remain hot for a long time and the Romans had to wear special shoes to protect their feet. In the colder provinces, richer Romans had heating in their houses. In Rome and elsewhere the baths were heated in the same way.

Roman Villas *Pages 78 & 79*	Comparisons are drawn through the completion of the table, between the features of a Roman Villa and a modern house belonging to a rich person. Fountain, well or spring - water feature in the garden or a pond Bath House - a swimming pool Mosaic - carpet Wall Plaster with painted frescoes - wallpaper Stone - brick walls Outbuildings, storerooms, offices - shed and garage Window shutters - curtains Hypocaust - central heating boiler / radiators Hearth or charcoal-filled brazier - microwave oven Hadrian's villa at Tivoli is near to Rome. It was a large country villa composed of a number of buildings, including a stadium, baths, libraries and a theatre. Acres of gardens surrounded it. The water features in the garden were decorated with sculptures of gods, people and animals, like crocodiles. *Page 79* - pupils are asked to draw comparisons between Celtic houses and Roman villas from the same period through imaginative writing. **Background Information:** Villas were luxurious self-sufficient country houses or farmhouses, set in gardens with pools, fountains and statues. They had ornate mosaics on the floors and walls and sometimes glass in the windows. Furniture was ornate and inlaid with ivory, marble or wood. The villas were made up of living quarters, storerooms, a bath house, stables, vegetable patches and orchards. Cereals, grapes and olives were grown on the land of the villa and were sold to make wine and oil. Meat, fruit and vegetables were used to feed the people who lived and worked in the villa but extra could also be sold. Meat could be obtained by killing animals (deer, boar, game) in the surrounding countryside. The land was irrigated so that it could drain properly and was fertilised with manure from the animals. Slaves carried out the farm labour.
Roman Mosaics *Pages 80, 81 & 82*	Following the co-ordinates carefully, a mosaic of a dog will be revealed. A mosaic like this would have been found at the entrance to a house. The Latin message reads CAVE CANEM - 'Beware of the Dog'. Pupils can make effective mosaics from small squares of coloured paper. The mosaic pattern ideas on *page 82* may be helpful. The *tesserae* can be stuck onto black paper. **Background Information:** Roman mosaics decorated the floors and walls (and sometimes the ceilings) of wealthy homes and public buildings and baths. Artists were highly skilled and made intricate pictures using thousands of tiny coloured stones or marble, called *tesserae,* which they pressed into wet concrete or plaster. Many mosaics have been excavated and give historians an insight into life in Roman times.

Roman Gardens

Page 83

Roman gardens were ornate and often had fountains. This activity shows the kind of plants and trees that the Romans had and how their gardens were organised. It allows for comparisons to be made with our modern gardens. When re-assembled, the jigsaw shows a picture of a typical Roman courtyard garden, with statues, water, flowerbeds, paths and lattice fencing.

This is how the garden should look.

Background Information:
Plants, particularly herbs, were used to make medicines. They were crushed using a pestle and mortar and made into pills, or added to wine to make linctus. Sage was grown and was used to treat sore throats, mustard and basil treated stomach-aches and headaches were treated with lemon balm.

Roman Citizens

Pages 84 & 85

These activity sheets draw comparisons between Roman citizens and British citizens today and pupils are asked to think of similarities and differences between them. The questions set are designed to instigate discussion and debate.

Background Information:
In the Republic, the time before the Emperors, Roman citizens were either *Patricians, Equestrians* or *Plebeians*. The former were the privileged class who claimed that their right to rule was due to being able to trace their ancestry back to the origins of Rome. The Equestrians were rich and the Plebeians were the ordinary working people. They formed an assembly which elected two and then later in history, ten tribunes, to represent their opinions in the Senate. The Senate made laws with the assembly. Two consuls were appointed and were guided by the Senate. During the Empire, Augustus, although he was sole ruler, maintained the structure inherited from the republic. He appointed consuls and senators.

Roman laws were created in 451 B.C. and were written on 12 bronze plates known as the Twelve Tables. These are among the first early examples of written law. The laws were refined by Emperor Justinian in A.D. 529 and they became known as the Justinian Code. These Roman laws formed the basis of today's justice systems.

Boys were trained to take their place as Roman Citizens and prepared for the task of ruling Rome and the Empire in the secondary school *grammaticus*. Here boys were taught public speaking if they wanted to be politicians or lawyers. They were taught by a rhetor how to write and present speeches and how to debate. As citizens, they were able to vote, but women and slaves could not.

A boy formally became an adult when he was about 14 years of age, normally after he had finished his basic education. A ceremony was held, when he went to the forum (an open space at the centre of Roman towns used for markets and trade) with his family and friends. There he removed his childhood clothes and bulla. He had his first shave, and was given a toga, which showed that he had officially become a Roman citizen. Afterwards, they celebrated the occasion with a party.

The Roman Family

Page 86

The sheet provides information on the Roman family. Comparisons can therefore be made between the Roman family and the modern family.

Background Information:
The average Roman family consisted of a father, mother, children, married sons, their family and slaves. The father *(paterfamilias)* had most power and was in charge of the household. Everyone had to obey his orders. When a child was born, the father of the house decided whether or not the baby should live. If children were not married by the age of 15 - 16 years, they were punished. Fathers arranged marriages for their children. The family gave a dowry of money to the husband when a daughter was married. The mother *(materfamilias)* had to obey her husband but she controlled how the house was run. Later, educated women held jobs as doctors and teachers.

Slaves were a very important part of Roman life. Some were born into slavery while many came from the provinces, captured in war. They were bought or auctioned at markets. Slaves were used in houses to cook, clean, or work the land. If they belonged to a good family they could receive money and could buy their freedom or they could even earn it. They became known as freedmen or women but they had no voting rights. Some slaves were well educated and others ran the family businesses or shops. A Roman was judged by the number of slaves he had. Other slaves had jobs as builders, labourers, rubbish collectors, road sweepers, gladiators, charioteers etc. Masters sometimes treated slaves harshly and brutally, punishing and whipping them.

Spartacus was the most famous slave who led a slave revolt in Southern Italy against harsh conditions and cruel masters. The army of 70,000 slaves was eventually crushed by the Roman general Crassus and 6,000 slaves were crucified.

Children and Education

Page 87

Many comparisons and contrasts can be drawn between the educational system in Roman times and today. The group-centred activities allow pupils to discover these similarities and differences, and, by reading and using the text, to imagine being in the shoes (or sandals) of a Roman child.
The Roman school report is a fun activity that works well and teaches pupils a functional style of writing.

Background Information:
In Rome, most people went to private school or studied at home. They studied reading, writing and arithmetic. Quite often Greek slaves taught pupils. They studied both Latin and Greek. Most schools only had one room and only one class of about twelve pupils.

They wrote on wax tablets *(tabulae)* using a stylus, or on pieces of pottery or on papyrus with ink. Books were scrolls. The cane was used to punish bad behaviour or poor work. At midday, children had a siesta to rest and avoid the midday heat.

Evidence from mosaics, sculptures and paintings has shown that children played many games. They had toys, such as wooden dolls, board games with glass, pottery or bone counters, kites, hoops, swings, metal chariots, stilts, rocking horses, dolls' houses etc.

Roman Numerals
 	
Page 88
	Roman numerals were useful in Roman times when merchants communicated by showing numbers with their fingers in order to trade with others from countries where they spoke a different language.
	
	Roman numerals used only seven letters to represent all numbers: -
	                I V X L C D M
	
	Letters are placed before or after each other to lower or increase their value:
	            IV = 4 XXIII = 23 MCM = 1900
	
	It was only in about 1500 that the Arabic number system (0-9) was adopted in Britain. However, Roman Numerals are still used today - on watches and clocks, at the end of films, on gravestones and for front door numbers etc.
	
	Answers to the numerals:
	    1. 22
	    2. 49
	    3. 74
	    4. 63
	    5. 86
	    6. 117
	    7. 299
	    8. 547
	    9. 777
	  10. 1900
	
	Answers to the sums
	    1. XI 2. XXI 3. IX 4. XCIX 5. CD 6. XX
	
	Pupils can work in pairs to make up their own numeral sums. It is best to practise by starting with simpler questions before trying more complicated ones. Many fun numeral games can be played with numeral dice. This could involve pupils making Roman numeral die using the nets of cubes.
	
	How to say the numbers:
	    1 unus (I) 8 octo (VIII)
	    2 duo (II) 9 novem (IX)
	    3 tres (III) 10 decem (X)
	    4 quattuor (IV) 11 undecim (XI)
	    5 quinque (V) 12 duodecim (XII)
	    6 sex (VI) 50 quinquaginta (L)
	    7 septem (VII) 100 centum (C)

The Latin Language

Page 89

Our alphabet today is based on the Latin alphabet. The letters **K, Y** and **Z** were not used very often. The letter **J** was the same as **I,** and **U** was the same as **V.** Capital letters only were used for names of people and places.

Latin was spoken in Italy and the educated also learned Greek. Latin was also spoken by the wealthy in the provinces. It spread to the provinces because it was spoken by the army, the governors and Roman officials. Latin had the greatest influence on languages in the West and many modern languages are based on Latin and its alphabet, such as French, Italian, Spanish, Portuguese and Romanian. Today Latin is not spoken any more, but is still commonly used in churches, in law and medicine. Some towns and schools have Latin mottos and most plants still have their Latin names.

This worksheet encourages the use of a dictionary.
Latin words:
1. **alter**native - choice between two things. When the choice lies with the other.
2. **sub**marine - under water, under the sea
3. **inter**national - between nations
4. **mal**function - working badly
5. **com**munication - exchange of message between people
6. **circum**ference - line around the circle

Abbreviations: -
P.S. - found as an addition at the bottom of a letter.
A.D. - the years after the birth of Christ
am - morning
pm - afternoon

Months of the year:
Januarius - named after Janus, god of the doorway
Februarius - named after a Roman purification festival *februa*
Martius - named after the god Mars. March for the Romans was always the first month of the year
Aprilis - when the flowers opened *'aperire'* (when the spring equinox fell)
Maius - of Maia, the mother of Mercury
Junius - named after the goddess Juno
Julius - named after Julius Caesar
Augustus - named after Augustus Caesar
September - seventh
October - eighth
November - ninth
December - tenth

Money & Trade *Page 90*	**Geographical skills** - this activity requires pupils to use the key to discover which produce came from different provinces in the empire. The writings by Cicero and Strato are primary sources and show the differing opinions of these two men about the produce from Roman Britain. **Background Information:** The more the Romans expanded their empire, the more goods were acquired and traded. For example, spices, amber and silks came from the Eastern empire. Spain supplied a variety of goods, like wool, cloth, silver, wax, olive oil, fruit, honey and fish. Greece supplied marble and purple dye and from Egypt came papyrus for making books and paper. Many items and goods were brought to Rome by boat. Boats were navigated by stars at night and sailed mainly in the summer, so as to avoid storms and being shipwrecked. The nearest seaport was at Ostia, which was about 15 miles from the city, and the goods were carried from here to Rome in barges up the River Tiber. They were stored in warehouses and were then sold to traders and the public. Boats carried food (grain and spices), amphorae and even wild beasts for the Roman entertainments. Under the emperors' reigns, the monetary system was standardised and all the coins had a fixed value. Emperors had a picture of their head on the coins. Goods were paid for using gold and silver coins and many have been discovered all over the empire in excavations.
Roman Clothing *Pages 91 & 92*	A fun activity allowing pupils to learn about Roman clothing, while dressing the family.
Roman Fashion *Page 93*	Roman fashion was very different from our fashion today and is an interesting topic for drawing comparisons. The activity of making Roman jewellery works very well and is fun. The end results are very effective on a display and if strong enough, can also be worn by pupils. **Background Information:** Clothes were generally made of wool or linen but sometimes silks. Vegetable and mineral dyes were used to brighten up natural colours of cloth. **Roman Men** Roman men wore simple loincloths for underwear. Over the top they wore knee-length tunics, fastened by a belt. They would wear *soleae* which were sandals worn inside the house and *calcei* which were heavier sandals for outside. On important and official days a Roman man would wear his white toga, which was made of fine wool. Black cloaks were worn for solemn occasions such as funerals. Roman men usually visited the barber for a shave. Cuts from blunt razors were very common and one remedy was to use spiders' webs soaked in oil and vinegar to stop the bleeding. **Roman Women** A woman wore a *stola,* which was a full-length fine wool or silk robe over simple underwear. The stola could be in bright colours, such as red, yellow or blue. She wore a *palla* over the top of a stola, which was a long rectangular scarf draped over her shoulders and sometimes her head. Her hair was always immaculately tied up with curls and scented. Hairpins held the hairstyles in place. To avoid dyes, sometimes women wore wigs from the hair of a slave - red or blonde were fashionable. She wore make-up and jewellery. Jewellery could be bought in shops belonging to gold and silversmiths. They made necklaces, earrings, hairpins, brooches, bracelets and rings. More ordinary jewellery was made of bronze, glass and coloured stones. Rich women had their make-up done by an *ornatrix* or make-up artist. White faces and arms were very fashionable and women used white chalk or lead to powder themselves. They used ash or squashed flies to darken their eyelids and eyebrows and they used plant dye or wine sediment to redden their cheeks and lips.

Food & Drink *Pages 94 & 95*	A menu for a Roman meal can be created from the ingredients in the basket, and from using the information page. **Background Information:** The Roman writer Apicus is the main source of evidence about Roman food and his recipe book is obtainable to buy. We can also find out more from excavations of animal remains and bones, olive stones and shells etc. and from wall paintings and mosaics. More exotic foods and spices became popular as the Roman Empire expanded. Romans tended to buy fast food from stalls on the streets as apartment blocks did not have kitchens. Food could be bought for cooking from markets. In Rome the markets were all over the city. Trajan built his market place very close to the forum. All foods could be bought here - fruit and vegetables, flowers, oil, vinegar, fish and meat. Food was weighed. Food did not last long before it started to rot, so strong sauces were created in order to disguise the taste of the old food. The process of wine making was learned from the Greeks. Cheap wine for the poor was called *acetum* and was declared 'unfit to drink' as it was so sour. Better quality wine was sweetened with honey. It was stored in pointed *amphorae* which were buried in the ground in order to keep the wine cool. The rich Romans loved to have banquets and large feasts. They would eat anything from three to ten courses. The Romans drank wine throughout the lengthy meal. They had a *vomitorium,* which was a room where they could be sick between courses, in order to create room in their stomachs for the next course of food! Entertainers, such as dancers, acrobats and jugglers, would entertain the guests, who reclined on couches, leaning on their left elbows. The guests ate with their fingers as the Romans did not have forks. Knives and spoons were used in the kitchens. Slaves would wash the guests' hands between courses. A good primary source for an exaggerated and vulgar Roman feast is Petronius' 'Dinner with Trimalchio' - *Cena Trimalchionis*. Here is a quote from it: *The next course to arrive - pastry thrushes stuffed with raisins and nuts. After them came quinces with thorns stuck into them to make them look like sea urchins. All this was fine if it had not been for another dish that was so horrible that we would have preferred to go hungry. It was put on the table looking like a fat goose surrounded by fish and all kinds of game . . . Trimalchio said, 'my cook made it all from pork . . . he can produce a fish from a pig's belly, a pigeon from the fat, a turtle dove out of the ham and fowl out of the knuckle.'*
The Theatre *Page 96*	The activity of making a dramatic mask works very well and is fun. The end results are very effective on a display and can also be worn by pupils to act out a play. **Background Information:** The Greeks originally built theatres and enjoyed plays. The Romans also adopted the idea and performed Greek plays but also wrote their own Roman dramas. They enjoyed comedies and also tragedies. Theatres were open-air buildings and consisted of an audience area, the orchestra (the space between the stage and the audience, where priests, senators and important officials sat) and a stage. The acoustics were always very good in the theatre. Women had to sit furthest from the stage area and awnings covered the audience to protect them from the sun. The audience became very involved in the action and screamed, hissed, booed and cheered. Riots could occur in the middle of a performance if there was a disagreement about the skills of different actors. The actors were always male and they wore masks so that it was easy to tell the character they were playing from a long distance. The masks had eye and mouth holes so that the actors could see and speak. Their costumes also explained their character. For example, slave characters wore plain tunics, the poor wore red costumes, the elderly wore white, purple was the colour of the rich and young characters had costumes of several colours. Musical interludes and accompaniment by cymbals, pipes, drums or singing often occurred as part of the drama.

The Races & Gladiator Fights	Entertainment in the amphitheatres and stadiums, known as *circuses*, became very popular. *Page 97* is an information page, and further research or a short project on the races and/or games could be encouraged. The primary sources on *page 98* show evidence of differing Roman opinions of the games and the activity demands interpretation of these writings.
Pages 97, 98 & 99	*Page 99* allows pupils to research the Colosseum in Rome (see notes below) and to make a fact book or guidebook.

Gladiator poster - information
The arched entrances on the Colosseum were numbered. Free tickets were given out on the morning of the show. The shows were spectacular events and were often held by ruling magistrates or at the expense of the emperor as a way of gaining votes in elections and popularity.

Background Information:
Chariot racing was the most popular form of entertainment and the Circus Maximus in Rome could have up to twenty-four races a day and could seat 250,000 spectators. Men had to wear their togas and the races were only for citizens and their families. Seating was in three tiers: senators on the first tier, less important citizens behind them in the second tier and the poorest citizens had to stand in the top tier, which was furthest away from the chariots. Unlike in the theatre and amphitheatre, men and women could sit together to watch the chariot racing. Emperors paid for the races as a way of gaining the people's favour. Race days were public holidays. In 4th Century every other day became a public holiday!

A chariot was a small cart, called a *biga,* which had two wheels and was pulled along by two horses. A three-horse team was called a *triga* and a four-horse team was a *quadriga*. It was a very dangerous activity because of the speed of the horses, and riders were often killed from colliding chariots or from being run over and trampled on if they fell. There were four teams: the Whites *(albati)*, Reds *(russati),* Blues *(veneti)* and Greens *(prasini)*. People supported one team and cheered them on, like our modern football teams. The Emperor Caligula supposedly was a supporter of the green team. Money was gambled on teams and charioteers. The horse-drawn chariots had to race around seven laps, covering about six miles. Each lap was counted with a golden marker that was turned on a rack. The winner won a palm leaf of victory and a large sum of money and became famous.

At the games
Gladiators were slaves, criminals or prisoners who were made to fight each other or wild animals in front of large crowds in the large amphitheatres. But some poor young men volunteered too, in the hope of winning fame and riches. If attending, the Emperor would often give a *thumbs up or thumbs down sign,* which would decide if the loser was to live or die.

There were fourteen types of gladiator, but the five main ones were:
Samnite (Samnis) - who had a sword, shield and helmet with a visor.
Murmillon - who had a sword, shield and a helmet crowned with a fish.
Thracian (Thrax) - who had a curved dagger and a small, round bronze shield.
Secutor - who had a sword, helmet, leg and arm guards. He fought the Retiarius.
Retiarius - who fought with a trident and a net. He had an arm guard on one arm.

Some gladiators became rich and famous but many did not live very long.

The Races & Gladiator Fights *Pages 97, 98 & 99*	Some Romans enjoyed watching animals fight each other to the death. The more exotic the animal, the more exciting the spectacle. Animals were brought from all over the empire to Rome and included lions, zebras, giraffes and elephants. Sometimes weaponless people, such as the Christians, were sent to the arena to face these hungry animals. Not all Romans enjoyed the gruesome entertainments and yet others were transfixed by them - as the primary sources indicate on *page 98*. St Augustine was a Christian bishop who lived from A.D. 354 - 430. Today Spanish bullfights are the closest that we can get to witnessing the Roman games. The most spectacular entertainment in the amphitheatre was the *naumachia* or sea battle recreations. This involved the flooding of the arena floor and used thousands of people. *Page 99* - The *Colosseum* - was a large stone amphitheatre (circumference 527m, height 57m) originally called the Flavian Amphitheatre as it was built under the reigns of the Flavian emperors. It became known as the Colosseum when Hadrian moved a statue of Nero, known as the *Colossus*, beside it. It could seat up to 50,000 spectators and was divided into three areas:- the *arena*, the *podium* and the *cavea*. The circular *arena* is named after *harena* (sand) which covered the central floor. This is where the spectacle took place. Underneath the *arena* floor were many passageways where cages and scenery were kept. The *podium* was a terrace on top of the arena wall where important people such as the Emperor or senators sat. They had the best view. The *cavea* was where the crowds sat. It was divided into three tiers, reached by stairs. Only men were allowed to sit in the bottom two tiers and women were separated and could only occupy the top tier. Large awnings were stretched out across the roof space in order to protect the audience from the sun or rain. The building was enormous but could be emptied within ten minutes owing to the large number of arched entrances and exits.
The Roman Baths *Pages 100, 101 & 102*	Hygiene and cleanliness were very important to the Romans and they made frequent visits to the baths to get clean, but also to socialise. **1 Flavius and Marcus visit the baths** **2 Apodyterium** was the changing room - it had no cubicles **(A)**. **3 Basilica** - next they went to this area where they played ball and wrestled **(B)**. **4 Tepidarium** was a warm pool where they rested after their exercise **(C)**. **5 Caldarium** was a hot pool in a domed room where they worked up a sweat. **(D)**. They were then cleaned by slaves with strigils. **(E)**. **6 Frigidarium** was an unheated, cool pool and was refreshing after the caldarium **(F)**. **7 Piscina** - was where they enjoyed a relaxing swim in the main pool before getting changed. **(G)**. | *Ancient Roman Baths* | *Modern Leisure Centre* | |---|---| | Basilica | Fitness area - exercise machines etc. | | Apodyterium | Changing rooms - with lockers and cubicles | | Frigidarium, tepidarium, caldarium | Showers and sauna | | Piscina | Swimming pool | | Market Hall | Cafeteria | | Food Stalls | Vending machines - with drinks and sweets | | Latrines | Toilets |

The Roman Baths

Pages 100, 101 & 102

Background Information:

Water was carried to the baths from the aqueducts and the sewers carried away the waste and overflow water. The baths were heated using the hypocaust system, where a furnace was burned under the floor and the hot air rising from it, heated the water. Men and women bathed at separate times and wore no clothing except for special shoes made of wood to stop their feet from burning on the floor. The Romans had no soap like ours but used oil on their skin which was removed by slaves scraping them with a *strigil*. This was a curved bone or wooden stick. Rich Romans had their own baths built in their villas. Some baths were ornately decorated with mosaics and pillars. Ancient Rome had eleven public baths or *thermae* and several privately owned baths which were only for the rich.

The most famous baths in Britain are at Bath in the southwest of England. It was known as Aquae Sulis in Roman times. Sulis was a Celtic goddess often associated with the Roman goddess Minerva. People came to swim here because of the medicinal waters, which they thought would heal their bodily complaints and illnesses. In Europe people still visit spas and other places believed to heal ailments - such as Lourdes in France. There are many spas in central Europe too - for example in Hungary and the Czech Republic.

ROMAN RELIGION

Roman Religion

Page 103

A *defixio* or *exsecratio* was a curse which was written down in a way that gave it a magical effect. It wished for evil to come to a person and the curser often addressed it to a god or goddess, begging for their support. Sometimes it was written with symbols.

Each word in this defixio is written in reverse to give it a more magical effect.

DEUS NEPTUNE
I CURSE HIM WHO HAS STOLEN MY CLOAK WHETHER MAN OR WOMAN SLAVE OR FREE. MAY NEPTUNE INFLICT ILLNESS UPON THIS MAN. MAY HE NOT SLEEP AT NIGHT UNTIL HE HAS RETURNED MY CLOAK TO YOUR TEMPLE.

Background Information:
The Romans believed in supernatural forces and worried about what the gods thought. There was a god or goddess for almost any activity and all of life was closely connected with religion. They were always anxious not to offend any god. Priests made sacrifices to the gods of oxen, goats, sheep, pigs, and doves on altars, to placate the deity. The Romans consulted the following experts: -

Haruspex was a priest who examined the entrails of sacrificed animals. If he spotted disease, it meant that the gods did not approve.
Augurs were prophets who made predictions from ominous signs in nature, such as lightning, cloud shapes, earthquakes and flocks of birds.
Sibyl was a prophetess who gave advice on interpreting the will and wishes of the gods.
Astrologers told a person's fortune by studying the position of the stars at the time of his birth.

Roman Religion

Pages 104, 105

Activities:
The questions on *page 105* are directly related to the family tree of the gods on *page 104*. This involves the interpretation of a family tree and the study of the relationships between the gods.

Answers:
1. Saturn and Rhea, known as Ops (who were brother and sister).
2. 2 brothers - Pluto and Neptune and 3 sisters - Juno, Vesta and Ceres.
3. Saturn, Jupiter and Vulcan.
4. Mars and Vulcan.
5. Diana, Apollo, Minerva, Mercury and Bacchus.
6. Sister
7. Brother - (actually they were half-brothers. Their mothers were Leto and Maia respectively).
8. Half-brother
9. Uncle
10. Mars, Venus, Vulcan, Diana, Apollo, Minerva, Mercury and Bacchus.
11. Venus, his sister
12. Mars
13. Cupid
14. Great grandson
15. Grandson

The activity on *page 106* teaches the specific titles associated with the state gods.

145

Roman Religion *Page 106*	**Answers:** JUPITER - Father of the gods JUNO - Goddess of women APOLLO - God of music and the sun MINERVA - Goddess of crafts and war MARS - God of war MERCURY - God of trade, messenger of the gods VULCAN - God of fires and forges VENUS - Goddess of love and beauty NEPTUNE - God of the sea PLUTO or DIS - God of the underworld VESTA - Goddess of the hearth CERES - Goddess of agriculture BACCHUS - God of wine DIANA - Goddess of hunting and the moon. **Background Information:** The Romans adopted the state gods from the Greeks but they changed their names. For example, Jupiter was the Greek god Zeus, Ceres was the Greek Demeter, Venus was the same as Aphrodite, and Juno was equivalent to Hera. The state religion was practised in public and every god had a special day which was celebrated. Many rituals were performed at ceremonies in front of the temples, where there was an altar. Here sacrifices were made. Anyone who wanted to make a specific request to the god or goddess was allowed inside the temple, which housed treasure, statues and gifts from worshippers. The main Roman gods were worshipped, together with the deified emperors and Roma, goddess of Rome.
Other gods *Page 107*	**Background Information:** The Romans worshipped and prayed to gods privately in their own homes at a *Lararium* or shrine. Every house had a spirit or *Lar* who protected the household. Small offerings of food and wine were given to the spirit. Each family had a *genius* or guardian spirit, *manes* or ancestral spirits and *penates* who were spirits of the storeroom. As the empire spread further to the east, the Romans adopted their exotic religions too. The cult of Mithras became popular amongst the Romans, as loyalty, courage and discipline were important. Mithras was a sun god who represented light, war, justice and faith. He was associated with the Greek god Helios and the Roman god Sol Invictus. In particular, soldiers were supporters of this religion. It promised life after death. Mithras is always depicted on relief sculptures as slaying the holy bull, symbolising giving life to the earth. The cult of Isis, from Egypt, was also very popular. She was the goddess of the earth and her worship involved exotic and elaborate rituals. It was only after the Emperor Constantine saw a vision that he was converted to Christianity, which resulted in an end to all persecution of Christians under his reign.
Christianity *Page 108*	The Primary sources show evidence of Roman opinion towards the Christian people at the time. Pliny's letter explains how he deals with the Christians and Trajan's reply is in agreement, although he insists that those who sacrifice to the Roman gods should be pardoned. Trajan tries to moderate Pliny's views in these quotes. **Background Information:** Christianity was not a popular religion as it posed a threat to the state religion and was monotheistic. Christians were tortured and killed if they refused to worship the Roman gods. The Christians and their supporters were persecuted throughout the Roman period but later it became the strongest religion. Christians met in secret in the underground catacombs of Rome and their sign was the **ICHTHYS** or fish symbol, which contained the name of Jesus. (The greek letters form an anonym which is translated as 'Jesus Christ, Son of God Saviour'). The Emperor Constantine was the first Christian emperor.

Symbols & Myths

Page 109

The Romans believed that certain gods represented different areas of life, and protected groups of people. For example, sailors were protected by Neptune, god of the sea, and women by Juno, the goddess of women and childbirth. Certain symbols are associated with the gods:

Trident - Neptune
Eagle - Jupiter (his other symbol was the thunderbolt)
Peacock - Juno (her other symbol was the pomegranate)
Winged boots - Mercury
Heart - Venus
Owl - Minerva
Bow and Arrow & Moon - Diana
Lyre and the Sun - Apollo
Spear - Mars
Hammer - Vulcan
Corn - Ceres
Hearth - Vesta

Research skills
This activity enables pairs or small groups to research information and relevant legends or myths about the gods, leading to group presentations. Comparisons can be made between the religions of the ancient and modern worlds.

Crossword

Page 110

Answers:

Across:
1. Mithras
4. Underworld
8. Diana
9. Mars
10. Sun
12. Jupiter
13. Christ
15. new
16. King
17. wine
18. clouds
20. Hearth
23. one
24. Haruspices
25. Vesta
27. Juno
29. sacrifice
32. sea
33. Emperors
35. Gaea
38. craft
39. Persia
41. throne
42. Heaven
43. goddess
45. moon
46. sister

Down:
2. Isis
3. hunting
4. Uranus
5. war
6. Dis
7. Venus
11. Ceres
13. Colosseum
14. Minerva
17. women
19. Rhea
21. soldiers
22. Neptune
24. Hades
26. trade
28. ox
30. Tartarus
31. temple
34. lions
36. Apollo
37. altar
40. forge
44. or

Death & Burial

Pages 111 & 112

Research skills:
This activity enables pairs or small groups to research aspects of the afterlife and leads effectively to group presentations. A book or display of the research about Roman death, mounted on black paper or card, looks particularly effective. Comparisons can be made between the ancient and modern worlds.

Background Information:
1. **Dis or Pluto** - was God of the Underworld and is also known as Hades. No temples were built or dedicated to him.
2. **Proserpine** - known as Persephone in Greek, was carried off by Pluto and forced to live half the year underground as she had eaten seven pomegranate seeds. She was queen of the underworld.
3. **Hades** - the name of the gloomy sunless place where souls went when they died.
4. **Tartarus** - a place of punishment in the Underworld for all evil-doers, where the souls of the wicked were tortured.
5. **Elysium** - a place of eternal happiness where the souls of the good and blessed went when they died. Known also as the Elysian Fields, the Champs Elysées in Paris are named after them.
6. **River Styx** - the river in the Underworld across which the souls of the dead were carried by boat after they died. The ancient people thought that the water was poisonous and where it poured down, it left the rocks stained black.
7. **Charon** - was the ferryman who rowed the souls of the dead across the River Styx. A coin was left in the mouths of dead people at their funeral. It was believed that this coin paid Charon the fare for the journey. In Virgil's Aeneid (Book VI) he describes Charon as having white unkempt hair and burning eyes.
8. **Cerberus** - the three-headed dog who guarded the entrance of the Underworld. He could be charmed by music or drugged with honey-soaked cake.
9. **Aeneas** - the hero of Virgil's Aeneid. In book VI he visits the Underworld where he meets people from his past (such as the unhappy soul of Dido) and his father Anchises, who is in the Elysian Fields and who foretells the future greatness of Rome.
10. **Sisyphus** - on earth he was a trickster and in Hades he was condemned to roll a huge stone endlessly up a hill to the top, although it always rolled down again.
11. **Tantalus** - on earth he stole the food of the gods and killed his own son Pelops, cooking his flesh for a banquet for the gods, who then brought the boy back to life again. His punishment in Hades was to stand in water up to his chin. He was 'tantalised' with food and water, which always moved out of his way when he reached out for it to satisfy his hunger and thirst.
12. **Tityos** - was punished and killed by the gods because he attacked Leto. In Hades he had his liver pecked at by two vultures.

Gravestones make good archaeological evidence and tell us much about the everyday lives of the Romans. Sculptural reliefs on the gravestones can tell us about Roman clothing, artefacts, hairstyles etc.

> To the spirits of the departed
> **FLAVIA DINYSIA**
> a very loyal wife
> is buried here
> she lived for 40 years
> Her heir set this up

Death & Burial *Pages 111 & 112*	**Background Information:** The mortality rate in Roman times was high, especially for women and children, and few people lived beyond the age of 50 years. Funerals were elaborate ceremonies and showed off the wealth and status of the relevant family. The body was carried in a procession (sometimes open with the corpse sitting up, so everyone could see it). The body was washed and rubbed in oil. An important person would be dressed in their state toga and the body would be covered in flowers and wreaths. It would lie in state for visitors to pay their last respects. A coin was placed in the mouth of the body, as the Romans believed that it would pay the ferryman Charon to carry the spirit across the River Styx to the Underworld. Cakes were sometimes placed in the hands of the dead person: these were intended to feed the three-headed hound Cerberus who guarded the entrance to the underworld. On arrival, the spirit would either go to *Elysium* (Heaven) or *Tartarus* (Hell) depending on the life they had led. A speech was made at the funeral, praising the dead person and then the funeral procession marched from the forum to outside the city gates, where graves lined the road. Each gravestone of the rich was carved with an aspect of their life. Professional mourners *(praeficae)* were hired to grieve at funerals. They carried a tear bottle in order to catch their tears and were paid by the quantity of tears that they shed and caught in the bottle. Romans were usually cremated, but some bodies were buried. Catacombs were filled with urns containing the ashes of the cremated.
The collapse of the Roman Empire *Pages 113 & 114*	This activity covers the events leading to and resulting in the collapse of the Roman Empire. Pupils are asked to illustrate the events outlined. **Background Information:** The Roman Empire came under many barbarian attacks and invasions which weakened the Roman defences and eventually brought about the collapse of the Empire and Rome itself. There were other reasons for collapse. Many of the soldiers in the army were paid foreign soldiers who did not show the same loyalty to Rome as the Roman soldiers in the earlier period. There was also endless infighting and Rome was spending too much money, more than it could afford, on trade and free rations. The Empire had also split into two - the east and west - under the reign of Constantine in A.D. 330. He moved his capital to the East and called it Constantinople. Alaric led the Visigoths to attack Rome between A.D. 408 & 410 and they established a city in Gaul (France). The Vandals and Goths conquered many of the southern provinces. The Vandals invaded Italy and attacked Rome in A.D. 455. Odoacer finally killed the last Emperor in the west and he reduced Rome itself to ruins. The eastern empire continued to survive until it was conquered in A.D. 1453 by the Turks.

What has changed and what has stayed the same?

Page 115

Our world would be very different if it had not been for ancient Roman civilisation. All over Europe the Romans founded cities which still stand today. These sheets lead pupils to understand the significant legacy left to the modern world by the Romans. It also allows pupils to understand the contrasts and differences between the modern and ancient worlds.

Main differences between life today and ancient Roman times:
Styles of clothes, religion - gods and worship, kinds of food, educational system, buildings, vehicles, different heating system, no electricity, gold and silver coins, monetary notes, political systems, army, language, toilets/bathrooms, slavery, games & entertainment, role of women etc.

Similarities between life today and ancient Roman times:

(i) **Public buildings** - hospitals, theatres and baths and also, glass windows and central heating.

(ii) **Coins** - and banking too. Coins were and still are minted.

(iii) **Architecture** - the Romans left the idea of building with stone and how to use and make concrete and cement. Many of our public buildings look a little like Roman temples and have columns. The arch was an important design still used today and we have inherited glass windows and central heating. They were the first to build buildings with several storeys.

(iv) **Numerals** - on clocks and watches and dates at the end of films are often written in Roman numerals.

(v) **Army** - the idea of an organised army where soldiers are paid comes from Roman times.

(vi) **Roads** - the network of roads built by the Romans has led us to continue to use them and to extend them, allowing greater ease of travel.

(vii) **Government and Law** - structured governmental system and laws come from the Romans.

(viii) Calendar - our calendar and our months of the year come directly from the Roman calendar - it was Julius Caesar's scientists who worked out the principles of our solar year.

(ix) **Planets** - the planets in our solar system are named after the Roman gods - Jupiter, Mercury, Venus, Uranus, Neptune, Saturn and Mars.

(x) **Language** - many Latin words and phrases still exist in English. See page 89. Latin is the basis of other European languages, such as Spanish, Italian, Portuguese and French.
- **Vice versa** - the other way round
- **Bona fide** - in good faith
- **Magnum opus** - great work
- **Compos mentis** - of sound mind
- **Nota bene (NB)** - note well

(xi) **Towns** - the Romans introduced the idea of urban living and town plans as well as a fire brigade under Emperor Augustus.

(xii) Christianity - was the official religion of the empire under the rule of Emperor Constantine. The Pope is the head of one section of the Christian Church and he lives in Rome.

The Legacy of Ancient Rome

Page 116

The Roman army withdrew from Britain in A.D. 410 to defend Italy from attack. Many parts of Roman life have survived through the centuries and feature in our lives today.

Answers to page 116: -
1. Roads
2. Postal system
3. Calendar
4. Language
5. Flats
6. Coins
7. Heating
8. Numerals
9. Arches
10. Toilets
11. Family
12. Towns

A collage of magazine pictures and drawings illustrating the legacy of Rome is a fun activity for pupils and an effective display for the classroom.

Historical References

British History

8 *In their study of British History, pupils should be taught about:*
  (a) the Romans
  (b) aspects of the histories of England, Ireland, Scotland and Wales, where appropriate, and about the history of Britain in its European and wider world context in this period.

Romans, Anglo-Saxons and Vikings in Britain

9 An overview study of how British society was shaped by the movement and settlement of different peoples in the period before the Norman Conquest and an in-depth study of how British society was affected by Roman settlement.

Key elements of History in the National Curriculum for Key Stage 2	Worksheet page number
Chronological understanding	
1a place events, people and changes into correct periods of time.	7, 8, 12, 13, 18, 20, 35
1b use dates and vocabulary relating to the passing of time, including ancient, modern, B.C., A.D., century and decade.	7, 8, 20, 33, 34, 35, 57, 113, 114
Knowledge and understanding of events, people and changes in the past	
2a characteristic features of the periods and societies studied, including the ideas, beliefs, attitudes, and experiences of men, women and children in the past.	20, 21, 22, 24, 25, 27, 28, 33, 34, 35, 36, 37, 84, 85, 86, 87, 91, 92, 93, 94, 95, 96, 97, 98, 99, 100, 101, 102, 103, 104, 105, 106, 107, 108, 111, 112
2b social, cultural, religious and ethnic diversity of the societies studied in Britain and the wider world.	10, 11, 13, 20, 21, 22, 27, 36, 84, 85, 86, 87, 103, 104, 105, 106, 107, 108, 109, 110
2c identify and describe reasons for, and results of, historical events, situations and changes in the periods studied.	10, 11, 13, 49, 53, 103, 104, 105, 106, 107, 108
2d to describe and make links between the main events, situations and changes within and across the different periods and societies studied.	20, 21, 22, 23, 113, 114, 115, 116
Historical Interpretation	
3 recognise that the past is represented and interpreted in different ways and give reasons for this.	1, 2, 4, 6, 27, 40, 45, 46, 47, 98
Historical Enquiry	
4a how to find out about the events, people and changes studied from an appropriate range of sources of information, including ICT-based sources.	1, 2, 4, 10, 11, 18, 42, 43, 44, 45, 46, 47, 48, 49, 50, 51, 52, 53, 74, 98
4b to ask and answer questions, and to select and record information relevant to the focus of enquiry.	1, 2, 4, 18, 36, 37, 39, 115, 116
Organisation and Communication	
5a recall, select and organise historical information.	1, 18, 36, 37, 39, 40, 46, 47, 48, 49, 50, 51, 52, 53, 110, 115, 116
5b use dates and historical vocabulary to describe the periods studied.	1, 2, 18, 33, 34, 35, 36, 37, 38, 39, 40, 51

Scottish 5-14 curriculum - Environmental Studies (Levels C - E) People in the past	Worksheet page number
Time and Historical Sequence	
Develop an understanding of time & how events relate in a chronological sequence.	7, 8, 18, 20
Explain the meaning of the terms B.C. & A.D., and the relationship between dates. Place events on a timeline to cross B.C./A.D. and in chronological order.	7, 8, 20, 35, 57, 113, 114
Knowledge and understanding of events, people & societies in the past	
Develop an understanding of distinctive features of life in the past and why certain societies, people and events are regarded as significant.	1, 18, 24, 25, 26, 27, 28, 33, 34, 35, 36, 37, 38, 50, 84, 85, 86, 87, 91, 92, 93, 94, 95, 96, 97, 98, 99, 100, 101, 102, 103, 104, 105, 106, 107, 111, 112
Explain the motives or actions of people in particular historical situations, the values & attitudes that characterised societies in the past & why they are of significance.	12, 13, 18, 20, 21, 22, 27, 28, 37, 45, 46, 48, 49, 50, 51, 53, 103, 104, 105, 106, 107
Study reasons why societies, people and events are thought to be of historical significance.	18, 20, 53, 72, 77, 88, 89, 115, 116
Developing understanding of change and continuity over time and of cause and effect in historical contexts.	
Identify important features of a development that have changed over an extended period of time. Explain why they were important and their effects on people's lives.	10, 11, 18, 20
Demonstrate knowledge & understanding of the main features of a particular event, development or circumstance, with regard to change and continuity. Explain why an event took place and the specific consequences.	18, 23, 45, 46, 47, 48, 51, 113, 114
Understand how decisions and events in the past can have significant effects on present circumstances or values.	10, 11, 72, 77, 88, 89, 108, 109, 115, 116
Developing an understanding of the nature of historical evidence - the variety of types of historical evidence and their relative significance.	
Develop the value of historical evidence. Explain the meaning of the term 'heritage' and give examples. Suggest ways that the past can affect the present and future.	1, 2, 3, 4, 9, 27, 108, 109
Skills - preparing, carrying out tasks, reviewing and reporting.	
Planning - in systematic & logical way. Identify appropriate sources of information. Carrying out - select relevant information, record in a variety of ways and evaluate. Reviewing & reporting - present appropriately & coherently. Present conclusions which are relevant for the purpose.	1, 3, 4, 9, 14, 18, 37, 39, 45, 46, 47, 48, 49, 50, 51, 52, 53, 110
Developing Informed Attitudes	
Importance of evidence/people in the past had different ideas from today.	1, 4, 30, 31, 45, 46, 52, 84, 85, 86, 87

Geographical References

Some elements of Geography in the National Curriculum for Key Stage 2	Worksheet page number
Geographical enquiry and skills	
1a ask geographical questions.	9, 16
1b collect and record evidence.	9, 78, 79
1c analyse evidence and draw conclusions.	9, 49, 54
2a to use appropriate geographical vocabulary.	5, 6, 9, 41, 65, 66, 67, 68, 69, 70, 71, 72, 73, 74, 75, 76, 77
2c to use atlases and globes and maps and plans at a range of scales.	9, 18, 20, 41, 54, 58, 59, 63, 66, 90
2e to draw plans and maps at a range of scales.	41, 58, 59, 65
2g decision-making skills.	16, 17, 80, 81, 82, 83
Knowledge and understanding of places	
3a to identify and describe what places are like.	9, 16, 17
3b the location of places they study and other significant places.	9, 16, 17, 20, 29, 30, 31, 32, 60, 61, 62, 63, 64
3c to describe where places are.	9, 16, 17
3d to explain why places are like they are.	29, 30, 31, 32, 53, 65, 66, 67, 68, 69, 70, 71, 72, 73, 74, 75, 76, 77, 100, 101, 102, 103
3e to identify how and why places change.	12, 24, 90
3f to describe and explain how and why places are similar to and different from other places in the same country and elsewhere in the world.	16, 17, 24, 91, 92, 93, 94, 95, 96, 97, 98, 99, 100, 101, 102
3g to recognise how places fit within a wider geographical context and are interdependent.	16, 17, 41, 60, 61, 62, 63, 64

Scottish 5-14 curriculum - Environmental Studies (Levels C - E) People and Place	Worksheet page number
Using maps	
Develop an understanding of location and features of maps.	9, 20, 54, 55, 58, 59
Using the main features from different kinds of maps.	9, 18, 20, 54, 58, 59
The Physical Environment	
Develop an understanding of the physical processes in the earth's surface . . . . climate, landscapes, physical processes.	41
Identify physical features, describe how people adapt to physical processes (climate).	19, 20, 21, 22, 23, 24, 25, 26, 27, 28, 29, 30, 31, 32, 53, 54, 60, 61, 62, 63, 64
Human Environment	
Develop understanding of patterns of human activity on earth . . . settlement, transport, and way of life.	3, 9, 16, 17, 60, 61, 62, 63, 64, 65, 66, 67, 68, 69, 70, 71, 72, 73, 74, 75, 76, 77, 83, 90, 91, 92, 93, 94, 95, 96, 97, 98, 99, 100, 101, 102
Give reasons for the location of settlements. Compare and contrast main features of lifestyle and population.	9, 16, 17, 28, 29, 30, 31, 32, 65, 66, 67, 68, 69, 70, 71, 72, 73, 74, 75, 76, 77, 91, 92, 93, 94, 95, 96, 97, 98, 99, 100, 101, 102
Human - Physical Interactions	
Develop understanding of the interaction between people and the earth's natural environment - land use, resources and change.	12, 16, 60, 61, 62, 63, 64
Describe the main features of common types of land use.	29, 30, 31, 32, 65, 66, 67, 68, 69, 70, 71, 72, 73, 74, 75, 76, 77
Skills - preparing, carrying out tasks, reviewing and reporting.	
Planning - in systematic & logical way. Identify appropriate sources of information. Carrying out - select relevant information, record in a variety of ways and evaluate. Reviewing & reporting - present appropriately and coherently. Present conclusions which are relevant for the purpose.	9, 30, 31, 32, 33, 34, 35, 36, 37, 38, 39, 40, 41, 53, 54, 55

Design Technology

During key stage 2 pupils work on their own and as part of a team on a range of designing and making activities. They think about what products are used for and the needs of the people who use them. They plan what has to be done and identify what works well and what could be improved in their own and other people's designs. They draw on knowledge and understanding from other areas of the curriculum and use computers in a range of ways.

Key elements of Technology in the National Curriculum for Key Stage 2	Worksheet page number
Knowledge, skills and understanding - Developing, planning and communicating ideas	
Teaching should ensure that knowledge and understanding are applied when developing ideas, planning, making products and evaluating them	
1a pupils should generate ideas for products after thinking about who will use them and what they will be used for, using information from a number of sources, including ICT-based sources	23, 42, 44, 82
1b develop ideas and explain them clearly, putting together a list of what they want their design to achieve	23, 42, 44, 82
1c plan what they have to do, suggesting a sequence of actions and alternatives, if needed	23, 42, 44, 55, 82
1d communicate design ideas in different ways as these develop, bearing in mind aesthetic qualities, and the uses and purposes for which the product is intended	23, 42, 44, 55, 82
Working with tools, equipment, materials and components to make quality products	
2a pupils should select appropriate tools and techniques for making their product	23, 42, 44, 55, 82
2b suggest alternative ways of making their product, if first attempts fail	23, 42, 44, 55, 82
2c explore the sensory qualities of materials and how to use materials and processes	23, 42, 44, 55, 82
2d measure, mark out, cut and shape a range of materials, and assemble, join and combine components and materials accurately	23, 42, 44, 55, 82
2e use finishing techniques to strengthen and improve the appearance of their product, using a range of equipment including ICT	23, 42, 44, 55, 82
Evaluating processes and products	
3a pupils should reflect on the progress of their work as they design and make, identifying ways they could improve their products	23, 42, 44, 55, 82
3b carry out appropriate tests before making any improvements	23, 42, 44, 55, 82
3c recognise that the quality of a product depends on how well it is made and how well it meets its intended purpose	23, 42, 44, 55, 82
Knowledge and understanding of materials and components	
4a understand how the working characteristics of materials affect the ways they are used	23, 42, 44, 55, 82
4b understand how materials can be combined and mixed to create more useful properties	23, 42, 44, 55, 82
4c understand how mechanisms can be used to make things move in different ways	23, 42, 44, 55
Breadth of study	
*During the key stage, pupils should be taught the **knowledge, skills and understanding** through:*	
5a investigating and evaluating a range of familiar products, thinking about how they work, how they are used and the views of the people who use them	42, 44
5b focused practical tasks that develop a range of techniques, skills, processes and knowledge	23, 42, 44, 55, 82
5c designing and making assignments using a range of materials	23, 42, 44, 55, 82

Scottish 5 - 14 Curriculum - Technology (Levels C - E) People in the Past	Worksheet page number
Knowledge, understanding, skills and attitudes - Needs and how they are met	
describe how effective designing and making takes account of how well products work	23, 42, 44, 55
Resources and how they are met	
show how the availability and properties of materials affect their use	23, 42, 44, 55, 82
demonstrate that materials and tools are resources necessary to make things	23, 42, 44, 55, 82
Preparing for tasks	
identify a problem, describe what needs to be done and give reasons for approaches	23, 42, 44, 55, 82
suggest and select information to decide helpful design criteria, based on observation and discussion and with relevance to potential users	23, 42, 44, 55, 82
develop and communicate a sequenced plan, individually and in groups, using appropriate media	23, 42, 44, 55, 82
Carrying out tasks	
use ideas, including any new suggestions, to represent a solution to a practical task	23, 42, 44, 55, 82
relate ongoing work firmly to design criteria, taking account of any necessary modifications	23, 42, 44, 55, 82
Reviewing and reporting on tasks	
suggest ways of gathering valid evidence to assess the quality of their work against design criteria	23, 42, 44, 55, 82
use observation and evidence from tests in identifying, suggesting and developing improvements	42, 44
record evaluative comment using a range of methods	23, 42, 44, 55, 82
show awareness of some consequences of their choices throughout a task	23, 42, 44, 55, 82
Developing informed attitudes	
creativity and skills, learning through practical experiences in a variety of contexts, as individuals and in teams	23, 42, 44, 55, 82
appreciating the impact of technology in society	23, 42, 44, 55, 82
respect the welfare and contributions of all interested parties, including when there are conflicting views	23, 42, 44, 55, 82
appreciating the contribution that technological activity can have	23, 42, 44, 55, 82